Peter Hartz

The Company that Breathes

Springer

Berlin
Heidelberg
New York
Barcelona
Budapest
Hong Kong
London
Milan
Paris
Santa Clara
Singapore
Tokyo

The author

Peter Hartz, Dr. rer. pol. h.c., was born on 9th August 1941 in St Ingbert/Saar. After initial training in industrial and business management he started a career in commerce. Since 1976 he has worked as a Human Resources Director first in the metalworking industry and subsequently in the Saarland steel industry.

With effect from 1st October 1993 Dr. Peter Hartz was appointed to the Executive Board of Volkswagen AG as Director of Human Resources.

The Company that Breathes

Every Job has a Customer

Peter Hartz

Springer

Published by Volkswagen AG, Wolfsburg
Editor: Helmuth Schuster, Wolfsburg

Translation from the German edition
„Das atmende Unternehmen" © Campus, Frankfurt/New York

ISBN 3-540-61315-3
Springer-Verlag Berlin Heidelberg New York

Cataloging-in-Publication Data applied for

Die Deutsche Bibliothek – CIP-Einheitsaufnahme
Hartz, Peter:
The company that breathes: every job has a customer/Peter
Hartz. (Publ. by Volkswagen AG, Wolfsburg). – Berlin; Heidel-
berg; New York; Barcelona; Budapest; Hongkong; London;
Mailand; Paris; Santa Clara; Singapur; Tokio: Springer, 1996
Einheitssacht.: Das atmende Unternehmen <engl.>
ISBN 3-540-61315-3

Translation: Hugh A. Keith, Edinburgh
Design concept and layout: Grandpierre & Partner Design, Idstein
Photographs: Marc Darchinger, Bonn
Production: PRODUserv Springer Produktions-Gesellschaft, Berlin

SPIN 10539441   68/3020 – 543210 – Printed on acid-free paper.

Contents

Foreword

This book contains a further development of the ideas found in the 1994 publication entitled "Every Job has a Face". It offers an initial overview of the new human resources and employment policy developed by Volkswagen which is at present the subject of so much international attention, and focuses on the scope for practical application and further development of the model. The texts of the new agreements signed within the company are included in the appendix.

The basic message of the book is a simple one: new solutions are possible.

It describes a revolutionary new approach exemplified by almost 100,000 individuals at Volkswagen in Germany. In today's world, terms of employment are more flexible and susceptible to faster change than many people might have expected. When jobs are at stake, employees' willingness to sacrifice income and make contributions themselves is greater than many might imagine.

There is greater scope for finding long-term solutions to employment problems via new working hours and wage arrangements than collective bargaining has acknowledged in the past. Such measures are not only justifiable in business terms but also practicable in reality. To deliver the sort of performance that assures a bright future, a company and its workforce must be capable of breathing. Towards the end of 1995 Volkswagen succeeded in achieving a "silent revolution". To our knowledge no other company had ever tackled so many sensitive issues – and successfully resolved them in a single blow.

All those involved were painfully aware of how crucial it was to have a major paradigm change if jobs were to be saved and Volkswagen was to continue to retain its company operations in Germany. What was needed was a completely new approach: a willingness to search for and find innovative and high quality solutions to our social problems fast. We have always been confident that the people in our company hold the secret of our success – a new willingness to reject rigidly fixed hours and to respond to the needs of the market, innovation cycles and performance-based objectives. A revolutionary new era is now dawning for the world of work. And at Volkswagen this means that almost 100,000 employees now have greater autonomy as far as their working hours are concerned and are more actively involved in teamwork.

The purpose of this book is to describe this revolution – to provide an enthusiastic account of what happened, and to pay tribute to the many people who have contributed to the success of the Volkswagen Model. My thanks are due to every one of them.

Peter Hartz
Wolfsburg, January 1996

Introduction

Maximise performance and productivity – optimise job security. This was the underlying objective of the 1995 round of collective bargaining at Volkswagen. It was an extension of the idea first introduced in 1993 with the 4-day week and described in the book "Every Job has a Face". How can one raise productivity and yet secure jobs, improve performance and yet assure levels of pay, enhance competitiveness and yet still retain expensive manufacturing locations? Once again, the question was directed towards the same 100,000 people who, in 1993, had opted for secure jobs and a 4-day week. So this time it was possible to draw on people's experience with that first experiment – was such an approach feasible in a sector which faces some of the fiercest global competition of any industry and bears such a heavy burden of high social standards as that in Germany?

The message coming from the VW experience is very clear: if you secure jobs by introducing variable working hours rather than layoffs, you can also preserve skills and maintain high levels of motivation within the company. Furthermore, you can also support the workforce in its efforts to achieve high productivity and enable cost adjustments to be made more rapidly than in the case of redundancy schemes. And yet this approach does not completely solve the problem of employment from the point of view of the company. In the long term, the "20% more employees and 20% fewer working hours" approach leads to higher unit costs, as statutory non-wage payments and job-related costs rise and fall with the number of employees, rather than with the volume of production. Furthermore, it is not possible to achieve 100% variability of wages directly related to working hour reductions. These two factors mean that the "residual costs" of offering job security have to be balanced by an increase in the performance – or the contribution –– made by the workforce. In order to achieve this further step towards achieving full competitiveness for the Volkswagen Model, it was necessary to radically restructure the company's compensation and human resources policies.

Thus any renewal of the promise to almost 100,000 people employed in the Volkswagen plants in Germany that they would not be condemned to layoffs under corporate downsizing schemes depended on being able to take a courageous step into the 21st century. Many taboos from the past had to be broken with:

• The contribution made by the workforce took an active role in the settlement achieved by collective bargaining. A performance increase of at least 4% had to be achieved by each and every group of employees. This meant that, on top of the 1994/5 drop in income of some 15% per head, yet further sacrifices had to be made in 1996.

• In addition to this, scope had to be created for productivity and human resource measurements to be determined on a more dynamic and competition-oriented basis which goes beyond traditional Methods Time Measurement procedures.

• The system had to offer scope for breathing by giving individuals greater freedom to determine their own working hours. Time corridors, time accounts, time credits, progressive timing, block working hours, and a degree of control over working hours derived from agreed performance standards and deadlines. Never before had the concept of working hours been opened up to such a degree.

• A new approach also had to be taken to remuneration plans. A uniform system based on performance criteria is now applied to white- and blue-collar workers alike. And scope has been left open for individuals to exercise greater control over their lifetime earnings – they have to ask themselves: "What do I want to receive today, and what will I put off until I retire?" The first step towards this new world was facilitated by the transformation of the present capital formation scheme into an additional personal pension plan.

- For all kinds of income safeguards – from short time work to early retirement – a new "acceptability curve" now applies. The principle involved is that the higher an individual's salary the more he (for the covenience of translation, the subject will be printed in the masculine form. This is not intended to be discriminatory or to cause offense) is expected to contribute to old-age provision. Gone are the times when mass solutions applied wholesale to everyone on the payroll.

- New ideas also had to be developed for improving mobility, flexibility and skills levels amongst the workforce. The ideas contained in the book "Every Job has a Face" took shape in the form of the Coaching Company, the Personal Development Plan, Personnel Deployment Operations and special promotion programmes for young managers using special selection criteria and tailor-made programmes for high-qualified. The opportunities offered to thousands of employees at Volkswagen have made the company into an important testing ground for a new approach to human resource management.

- It is also the duty of a company to try to create new jobs. Complaining about Germany's disadvantages as a location for industry achieves nothing. The scope for management and employees to create new, competitive jobs needs to be thoroughly explored. This, too, is one of the themes of this book.

All this sounds rather easier than it actually is in practice. And there is no intention here to gloss over the difficulties involved. Indeed, to achieve the intended changes, the employers had to take the unusual step of entering the annual round of collective bargaining with a complete package – including a list of demands which had to be made of the workforce.

This was the unique thing about what happened at Volkswagen. For the first time, the company was putting forward an entire, complete strategy – a package which took into account the interests of the employees, but redefined priorities, putting the spotlight on securing jobs, balancing workforce adjustments with progressive work reduction programmes and introducing participative pensions to fill the expected gap in old-age provision. At the same time the company's approach succeeded in strengthening Volkswagen's competitive position within Germany. The concept of a demand-driven, breathing company was underpinned by the introduction of the Volkswagen Week, greater individual control over working hours with a focus on functions and performance objectives, and a reassessment of manpower requirements based on group work. A convergence of interests had been achieved.

Despite all this, feelings ran high and the slow progress between the two negotiating parties was accompanied by demonstrations and walkouts. Compromises cost money – but the money was threatening to evaporate as a result of loss of production and market share. It required considerable determination on both sides for the problems associated with 38 parallel collective agreements finally to be solved. The complexity of the negotiations and the compromises put forward were such that informing and convincing both management and trade unionists became a marathon communications task.

This book will also look at the aspect of co-determination. Both sides are ultimately only as good as their ability to achieve consensual support for company strategies in difficult times. Both sides had their doubts – and there was considerable temptation to let the whole affair deteriorate into a struggle along classic lines. However, if a new "alliance for jobs" is to develop, then it is vital to be able to take a different view of things, to achieve credibility. In these rapidly changing times, it is not necessarily more socially responsible to defend past achievements in the social sphere than to take positive action to help maintain competitiveness.

Alternative routes to more jobs are few and far between. In most cases other companies "committed to fighting unemployment" are doing their best to achieve similar goals – and we are not suggesting they should cease their efforts. Nobody claims to have found the ultimate solution. But neither can anyone withdraw into playing the role of the victim – now that it has become clear just how much can be achieved – as an individual, a company, a workforce, a trade union, an association – and as a policymaker.

The ambitious aim of any "alliance for jobs" has to be that of reducing the strain on the labour market and creating new employment opportunities. No social policy or competitive strategy should be ignored, no geographical or labour policy opportunity passed over.

Directly or indirectly, every seventh job in this country depends on the German automotive industry. And, according to the German Automotive Industry Association, every fifth Deutschmark of tax revenue in Germany is derived from cars – their manufacture or their use.

This socially significant role of the German automotive industry is well worth protecting against the challenges of global competition. However, for far too long this has been regarded purely as a technological and financial challenge. The Volkswagen Model will have achieved much if it demonstrates the contribution which can also be made in the sphere of human resources.

The new concept of acceptability

Responding to competition, maintaining company locations and furthering the transformation process

In the long term, the only safe jobs are competitive ones – and the challenges are increasingly taking on global proportions. Jobs in Germany will only survive if they can be put on a new basis. We need to view our own situation in a new light and find different solutions by changing our frame of reference. A new concept of "acceptability" offers a way for traditional industries in high-cost locations to survive the future.

Acceptability – the key to new solutions

1993 was a year of change – a year characterised by a new-found courage to take on board new ideas, try out different approaches, face up to awkward decisions. It was a year which saw the introduction of new developments such as the 4-day week and other innovative approaches to work organisation. The key concept of "acceptability" swept aside the rigid divisions and taboos which had hindered the finding of solutions to the employment crisis at Volkswagen. Few people imagined it would be possible to break away from the traditional response to problems whereby a minority was sacrificed in order to save the majority – which in labour market terms always means dismissing a small section of the workforce in order to be able to guarantee full employment to the remainder.

Prior to the introduction of the Volkswagen Model, few people imagined it would be acceptable to the workforce and feasible for the management to achieve instant, massive savings in human resources costs and still avoid dismissals – simply by a redistribution of time.

Now, after two years of discussion – in both Germany and Europe – it has become clear that we have succeeded in raising the principle of security of employment onto a new plane. However, a realignment of interests to the benefit of everyone concerned only occurs if words are followed by actions. Too many policymakers, employers and trade unionists still tend to cling to their traditional beliefs and have only been prepared to take a cautious first step – promising more provided the other side moves first – and always with the threat of falling back with a vengeance into their old, entrenched positions if the other side fails to deliver the goods and negotiations break down!

The discussion about an "alliance for jobs", which arose in early 1996, must not be allowed to degenerate into the familiar scenario whereby slow progress is made, but with everyone still facing backwards. This is where the "new acceptability" comes into its own: instead of clinging to principles, it offers us a chance to move towards greater flexibility, to create openings where in the past there were only barriers – to build bridges. Over every horizon there lies new territory – but you must be able to see beyond the end of your own nose to realise this.

"Acceptability" is the new concept which, two years ago, entered the debate as the key to a radically different approach to social policy. It has much to offer:

- Personal initiative: the starting point is the individual
- Personal involvement: everyone is prepared to play a part
- Fairness: everyone contributes according to his capabilities
- Action: material and functional, mobile and social – starting points to demonstrate willingness to change
- Time – it makes things more acceptable. It is better to wait, hold back, introduce short-term measures, find temporary solutions rather than endanger everything by refusing to let go of an idea
- Dynamism: acceptability allows the creation of new terms of reference and new standards – leading to new expectations and values
- The impossible: convergence and consensus can be achieved, even where one partner has all the advantages and the other all the disadvantages. The acceptability formula which means there are neither winners nor losers goes as follows: swap one person's major disadvantage for another person's minor advantage! Convert an "acceptable" disadvantage into a comparative advantage!
- And, finally, ethics: acceptability means that – even where the harshest measures and the toughest competition are involved – social responsibility remains. Competition does not force unethical behaviour.

It is important to grasp this basic point, for many of the Volkswagen solutions involve exploring fully the scope offered by this new acceptability. The extent to which this involves compromises, based on the ability of individuals and groups to take on burdens, can be seen in the new terms which have been coined: the "acceptability curve", which always ensures that a heavier burden is put on the shoulders of those who earn more; or the "flexibility cascade", which categorises all working hours according to acceptability, establishes priorities for their flexible use and only as a last resort involves less popular measures such as night-time or Saturday working.

This was the major challenge faced by those who were to implement the new concept – how to apply the new values and new relationships in such a way as to get more out of traditional terms of employment, achieve greater variability and responsiveness of working times, and persuade those involved to abandon tradition and accept a more flexible and dynamic approach to their working lives. This was the threshold which had to be crossed.

Acceptability from the point of view of those affected

How well did this concept of acceptability go down with the workforce? Has the Volkswagen Model really succeeded in redefining what is "acceptable"? To what extent is the workforce prepared to support this new approach to human resources and employment policy?

Sample surveys carried out amongst the German public by the FORSA opinion research institute (1995) and at VW AG (2,600 respondents from a cross-section of the workforce, May/June 1995) by the Sociology Institute of the University of Erlangen/Nuremberg as part of a project run by the Hans-Böckler Founda-

---

Acceptance of the Volkswagen Model
Reduction of working time and salary while retaining jobs

Public opinion	**Opinion of workforce**
Is the Volkswagen Model suitable for securing jobs?	How satisfied are you with the 28.8-hour week?

Public opinion	Opinion of workforce
	Very dissatisfied **5 %**
No **20 %**	Dissatisfied **11 %**
Don't know **29 %**	Both **35 %**
Yes **51 %**	Satisfied **39 %**
	Very satisfied **10 %**

Source: FORSA   Sociology Institute, University of Erlangen/WSI, Düsseldorf

tion, indicate a high degree of acceptance. 51% of German employees regard the Volkswagen Model as being an appropriate method of securing jobs, whereas 29% reject the linking of reduction of income with reduction of working hours. Among VW employees 49% are either "satisfied" or "very satisfied" with a 28.8-hour working week combined with a 15% reduction in material benefits, and only 16% appear to be "dissatisfied" or "very dissatisfied".

This high degree of acceptance has been achieved despite the fact that a majority of the workforce – 53% – regard the financial constraints resulting from a 4-day week as "severe" or "very severe". How has this been done? The principle reason is that jobs have been made secure – a fact ranked at the top of the list of advantages of the new model by 74%. And there is agreement on this throughout the workforce. Blue- and white-collar workers, men and women, high and low wage categories – all ranked job security at the top of the list. After a mere one and a half years of operating the new system, such a result is in some respects surprising – given that the Volkswagen Model caused considerable shock waves when it was originally put to the workforce and met with a high degree of scepticism.

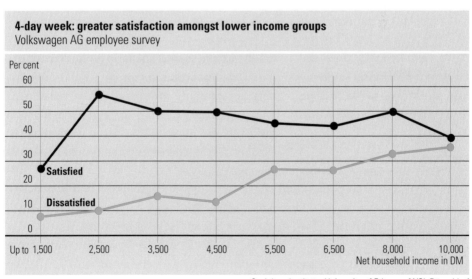

4-day week: greater satisfaction amongst lower income groups
Volkswagen AG employee survey

Per cent

Satisfied

Dissatisfied

Up to 1,500   2,500   3,500   4,500   5,500   6,500   8,000   10,000
Net household income in DM

Sociology Institute, University of Erlangen/WSI, Düsseldorf

Nevertheless, views on acceptability do differ to some extent. One unexpected finding of the survey was the extent to which the degree of satisfaction with the Volkswagen Model correlated with level of income. It had been expected that those on higher salaries would be happier than those with below-average net income. But the opposite is the case. The proportion expressing their satisfaction with the situation reduces relatively steadily from 60% amongst the lower wage groups up to 36% amongst the higher salaried groups. Despite their general acceptance of the model, the older, higher-qualified members of the workforce are clearly less satisfied than the younger ones. And women view the model more favourably than men.

The high degree of acceptance amongst those less able to absorb reductions in income – especially those on the lowest wages – offers striking proof of the importance of the concept of "acceptability". Even where hard material facts would seem to speak against a measure, there can be a high degree of agreement if a new balance of acceptability can be found.

This result suggests that, even in other sectors with a less favourable starting-point than Volkswagen, there is far greater scope for redefining acceptability than many people had imagined. It is important that social policymakers should draw on this hitherto untapped source of solutions in their attempts to ensure that more people are able to face a future in employment.

By the end of 1995, the new models for working hours had made it possible to keep on 20,000 more people than expected.

Prognosis and reality: scenario for further action

One important factor in establishing the new acceptability is credibility. All statements and predictions relating to future employment problems and opportunities must be credible. In October 1993, when the company management presented its employment analysis for Volkswagen AG's six German plants, and spoke of layoffs of 30%, or 31,000 employees, there were those who labelled this "scaremongering" and claimed that things would not turn out as badly as predicted.

However, the prognoses came true. Stagnating sales, coupled with accelerating productivity levels, completely confirmed the demand forecasts of 1993. The actual average working week, including overtime, was between 28.8 and 30 hours per capita. Just under 14,000 employees have now left – or are about to leave – the company under structural short time work and early retirement programmes. And over 2,000 apprentices and junior staff have been taken on in full-time jobs.

The bottom line is that – in rare confirmation of the forecasts made in 1993 – the same volume of vehicles is now being manufactured as before the measures were introduced in 1993 – but

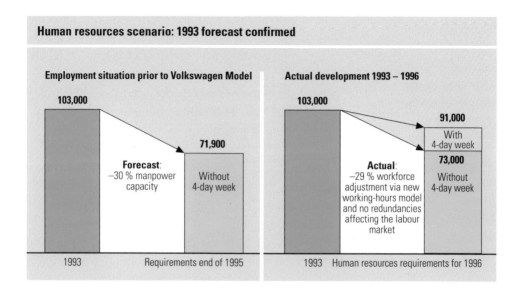

Human resources scenario: 1993 forecast confirmed

Employment situation prior to Volkswagen Model

103,000

71,900

Forecast: –30 % manpower capacity

Without 4-day week

1993   Requirements end of 1995

Actual development 1993 – 1996

103,000

91,000

With 4-day week

73,000

Actual: –29 % workforce adjustment via new working-hours model and no redundancies affecting the labour market

Without 4-day week

1993   Human resources requirements for 1996

with personnel reduced by 31,000 man-years! It is an astonishingly precise achievement – the result of 24 months' concerted effort to bring the employment problem under control without adversely affecting the labour market!

To what extent will the pressure for acceptability increase – what further strain is likely to be put on the goodwill of all those concerned? Have Volkswagen's initial, drastic measures left any scope for applying the principle of acceptability to combating even stiffer competition and higher costs? How far can one go in demanding even greater efforts on the part of the workforce to reduce costs and increase productivity? What are the new scenarios? Is there any future for Volkswagen's manufacturing operations in Germany? Has the situation been brought under control, or is it likely to worsen? Is the pace of change accelerating, and are the demands made on the quality of our work increasing still further? Will we be able to keep up with the pace, or do we need to make a new quantum leap in terms of acceptability? Or – to put it more provocatively – should not the entire workforce be putting in a 40+ hour week as though their jobs depended on it – but for pay based on a 4-day week?

It was important first to examine these questions in depth. What then followed was that the Volkswagen Model was further developed and turned into an all-embracing, comprehensive concept. It is the purpose of this book to explain the concept, and to describe the experience gained over the first 24 months of its implementation.

The three main objectives which the extended Volkswagen Model has to support are: maintaining global competitiveness, safeguarding the future of production locations by long-term cost improvement, and controlling and accelerating the process of change within the company. Any concessions made on the collective-bargaining front must not be allowed to endanger these objectives. They constitute three vital contributions towards maintaining levels of employment.

Competitiveness vis-à-vis the customer means not missing out on a single person who wishes to buy a product from the company. The statement "Actually, what I really wanted was a Volkswagen ..." should never be heard again. The system of working hours and human resources management should be able to respond instantly to the market – to breathe. The customer can then be supplied within 14 days, agreed deadlines can be met, and surges in demand or new sales opportunities can be translated into increased jobs. One of the central objectives of the 1995 round of negotiations was to provide a basis for creating a "company that breathes".

Price, quality and service must be totally competitive on a global scale.

If our avowed aim is to secure the future of all the company's manufacturing locations in Germany by achieving long-term cost reductions, then this means that no single location is going to be given up without a fight. The preambles to Volkswagen's 1993 and 1995 collective agreements contain a joint commitment to this principle on the part of the company and the IG Metall trade union. We take a realistic view of German – and European – manufacturing locations, because we want to build cars here. We do not want to transfer yet more operations to foreign locations based on cost. It is therefore vital that Germany's cost disadvantage vis-à-vis other possible locations should not increase. Indeed, the gap must be narrowed – because Volkswagen intends to vigorously defend the present quota of 58% German jobs within the Group. Decisions on where to locate operations should not be hampered by wage policies and the burden of social costs. Provided cost improvements can be agreed on, there is scope for expanding employment in the company's traditional locations – and this can also be justified in terms of corporate strategy.

For the company to survive it is essential to guide and accelerate the process of transformation. In an era in which expectations and the operating environment are changing increasing rapidity, all one can do is to set interim goals and do one's utmost to achieve these before anyone else does. Coping effectively with change has become one of the major functions of management. Since May 1994, all managers in the Volkswagen Group have had to be committed to helping achieve a rapid and radical change in attitudes and patterns of behaviour. Securing jobs and setting employment targets have to become part and parcel of the company's vision and strategy. There must be a clear awareness within the company that higher levels of employment are desirable – and that specific efforts are being undertaken to make this economically viable.

The order of the day for the leading-edge employer must be to develop jobs with long-term job security.

Increasing competitiveness – maintaining company locations – achieving successful change: How strong are the others?

Competitiveness – the key to a secure future

Profit margins of 4% to 8% are perfectly feasible at the top end of the automotive industry – but Volkswagen's margin is still under 1%, despite the massive improvement achieved since the all-time low of 1993. In other words, the processes taking place within the company still almost swallow more money than they generate. Profitability is a useful indicator of competitiveness,

23

and the above figures reveal that international competitors still seem to have greater scope for innovation and investment – and also more room to manoeuvre in a crisis. If the latter is lacking, then fewer resources become available for investment in products and processes for the future – and it is these which ensure competitiveness and, ultimately, secure jobs.

The result is a vicious circle of poor competitiveness. And if you resist the pressure to remain competitive, and transfer your costs into your prices, you lose market share and sacrifice more and more jobs. If you react to this by reducing profit margin per unit in order to maintain your market share, then – if you do not take any other measures – you slip into a permanent state of poor profitability which can endanger your entire operation and result in job losses. If you try to take positive action and develop a counter strategy, you cannot avoid reducing your costs and introducing rationalisation mea-sures: personnel costs, process costs (manufacturing time and depth), product costs – all must be reduced. The bottom line is: reduce costs or lose jobs.

The development of a strategy to ensure employment and a coherent human resources policy is essential.

Thus the problem of employment and human resources is closely related to the question of competitiveness. The more rationalisation objectives can be achieved, the lower the manpower requirements, and the greater the chance of achieving higher business volumes – which means increased manpower requirements. In the case of Volkswagen, the chance of expanding the volume of business via higher levels of employment doubles if 100% – rather than 50% – of rationalisation objectives are achieved. However, the achievement of rationalisation objectives reduces manpower requirements more drastically than can be compensated by the resulting growth in business volume. The extent of the effect may differ from case to case and sector to sector – but one thing is always true: if competitiveness is not maintained, the situation deteriorates even further.

No company, no union, no government can operate a successful employment and social policy without taking this mechanism into account.

Tangible cost improvements to safeguard company locations

One further insight emerges: if you wish to safeguard the position of a particular manufacturing location, it is vital to sign a specific agreement for that location, so as to reduce cost gaps and eliminate disadvantages of up to 50% in costs and quality compared with the world's most favourable locations. Once a location begins to fall behind the rest, it is extremely difficult to make up the lost ground, as the best competitors will continue to improve and will be joined by many more "greenfield locations" with state-of-the-art technology and no legacy of past problems.

However, even if complete profitability is achieved, this is not enough to ensure that a location will be saved and levels of employment maintained. In the case of the automotive industry in Germany, measures to improve the competitiveness of the product in the market are not in themselves enough to guarantee that levels of employment will be maintained.

In addition to the traditional methods of achieving adjustment, new, innovative ones also need to be found. Otherwise the market situation alone – with low-cost regions returning the highest growth, overall growth rates remaining relatively low, more vehicle and higher specifications being available for the same money, manufacturing depth continuing to decrease, and pressure mounting to improve productivity – will be enough to ensure that job losses continue.

You will only succeed in maintaining a traditional company location if you are able to use your human resources as flexibly and efficiently as possible to create new employment opportunities – and if statutory and negotiated terms of employment support you in doing so.

Volkswagen has defined six areas in which employment targets for its German manufacturing locations are being systematically developed. These include insourcing through the integration or setting up of new manufacturing capacity as part of future product developments; extending the product range into niche markets or new product segments; achieving increased sales of components, engines and units that are in high demand, and re-investing profits to extend existing technological leads; using every additional opportunity to expand business volume by develop-

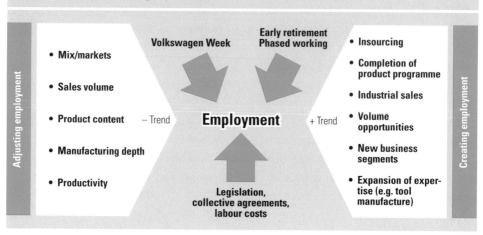

Human resources scenario: new models for employment and working hours help safeguard company locations

Adjusting employment

- Mix/markets
- Sales volume
- Product content
- Manufacturing depth
- Productivity

– Trend

Volkswagen Week

Early retirement Phased working

Employment

+ Trend

Legislation, collective agreements, labour costs

Creating employment

- Insourcing
- Completion of product programme
- Industrial sales
- Volume opportunities
- New business segments
- Expansion of expertise (e.g. tool manufacture)

ing Volkswagen into a company that breathes; enhancing the competitiveness of in-company expertise and services, for example, in tool manufacture within the Group, and developing new strategic business segments for the future of transport systems centred on the car.

The situation calls for a radical rethink. The employees and their representatives are actively involved in identifying where the potential lies and how it can be consolidated. This is where the VW Works Councils come into their own.

Steering and accelerating the process of corporate transformation

Speed is of the essence when ideas or measures are being developed and implemented. The experience of other sectors teaches us that this is one of the most important factors in maintaining employment.

If you are always first in the market, or your high productivity means your products are better value than anyone else's – or you are ahead of the rest of the field in technological terms – it is possible to actually increase employment levels, despite having improved productivity by 100% in four years and operating with

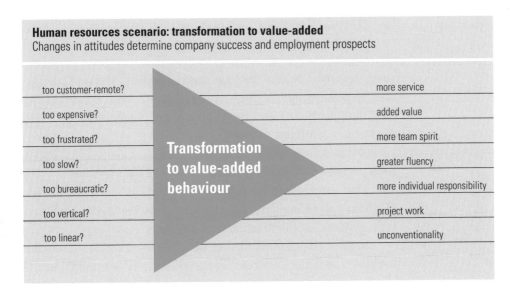

Human resources scenario: transformation to value-added
Changes in attitudes determine company success and employment prospects

too customer-remote?		more service
too expensive?		added value
too frustrated?	**Transformation to value-added behaviour**	more team spirit
too slow?		greater fluency
too bureaucratic?		more individual responsibility
too vertical?		project work
too linear?		unconventionality

six-monthly product cycles. Faced with the sheer speed of change in the automotive industry, a company like Volkswagen can easily start trailing by 80% or more if it does not manage change skilfully. But, if managers and the workforce can change their way of thinking faster than anyone else, if their basic attitudes can be better geared to productive and focused patterns of behaviour than elsewhere, then it is possible to establish a time lead and leave the competition behind.

Converting requirements into acceptable changes

Maintaining competitiveness, retaining manufacturing locations and transforming the company are all processes which require considerable effort on the part of those concerned – management, workforce, unions and legislators – if employment objectives are to be achieved. All are able to influence the outcome and can, by their behaviour, widen or narrow the chances of success. Everyone has something to contribute.

Many recent developments have seriously blighted Germany's attractiveness as a location for manufacturing operations. Economic growth without the creation of new jobs has brought German unemployment up to a record level of 10% – high by European standards. Labour costs and additional, non-wage costs are now amongst the highest anywhere in the world, and the situation is getting worse. Every year, the German social security budget outstrips the investment budget of German companies by several billion Deutschmarks. Taxes and social security contributions have now topped 40% of net business output – and the burden continues to grow.

Each person's contribution – the possible and the essential

Discussion about the future of jobs and the increased burden of labour costs should not be allowed to hide the fact that one can contribute to finding acceptable solutions.

Why can we expect further progress to be made in enhancing competitiveness, increasing the attractions of manufacturing locations and achieving the transformation of companies? As work nowadays has become more humane, it occupies a smaller part of our lives and offers us greater autonomy – with the result that demands for flexibility, variability and mobility are much more acceptable than they were in the past. There is greater scope for different life patterns. As the net sacrifice by the worker in terms of higher performance or lower income growth is less than the gross burden of employment which the company has to bear and recoup by rationalisation of work processes. Thus, the prospects in terms of wealth for employees after 50 years of peace, property-owning and full social security offer a much more stable basis for acceptability than could have been imagined some years ago. Every year a total of DM 200 billion – on average DM 200,000 is passed on from one generation to the next in Germany. In addition, the life-insurance companies pay out some DM 25 to 30 million every year to the older generation. This decade, some DM 500 billion in real estate will be passed on to the next generation.

A new era is dawning that offers people more scope for alternative life patterns.

Many of the burdens which people complain about do not have to be as onerous as people claim they are. Take, for example, continuation of wages in case of illness. With a working week of 35 or 28.8 hours and 42 days paid time off plus statutory holidays per year, it is now rather more reasonable to be expected to look after one's health and use the scope offered by 168 flexible working hours to put in the 35 or 28.8 that one needs each week. If you are healthy, you turn up and don't let your team-mates at work down. If you are ill you receive full benefits. If everyone lived according to this idea of acceptability, the debate about continuation of wages in case of illness would solve itself without any need to change the law. Managers and works councils can themselves raise the state of the workforce's health to 97% or better if they succeed in changing attitudes at local level.

Many processes could be made to run more smoothly. Access to the labour market, for example. If an apprentice realises that his training involves investment of well over DM 1 million in subsequent employment in industry, he is likely to accept many more demands in terms of initiative, mobility and personal contribution than in the past.

An intelligent approach to problem-solving is the name of the game. The "alliance for jobs", whatever the scale, can be pieced together from many individual elements – job by job, commitment and targets, laws and agreements – a wide variety of different approaches is conceivable.

The essence of Volkswagen's human resources policy is: encouraging the sort of performance which enables security to be offered in return.

The company that breathes

How a modern company is driven by people and markets

A world-class corporation group re-defines itself as a "company that breathes", dedicating its operations worldwide to meeting the needs of the customer. It does so by applying a revolutionary concept which combines total customer-orientation with a strong focus on value-added processes, supported by skilful change management.

Total customer-orientation

Successful companies are driven by people and markets. The very best companies are able to combine both elements: a workforce which is enthusiastic about the customer and, consequently, customers who are enthusiastic about the company. Top-class companies are even able to keep pace with changing customer requirements and developments on the market. All their processes and resources are designed to breathe – from the product development cycle right down to the delivery speed. The concept of breathing takes lean manufacturing to its logical conclusion and applies it to the entire company. All process times are shortened. No customer – and no market – can make this sort of company short of breath. This is "customer service" taken to its ultimate conclusion. And the customer responds by buying the company's products.

The vision of a "company that breathes" in response to the market's requirements provides the basis for a proactive human resources and employment policy.

This is a dynamic vision: it involves actively approaching the customer. It is also a clear vision: customer enthusiasm is the aim. Let us look at an example of the breathing company of the future: the salesman visits the customer at home and using his laptop with CD-ROM and cyberspace, introduces him to the range of products available and offers him a test drive. The salesman can then put together a complete package, including finance, and have delivery confirmed via a data check, if required. This is the 2-2-2 approach: within two hours the customer can have the car from the dealer's showroom, within two days from the regional distribution centre, and within two weeks a custom-built vehicle from the factory.

If the contact with the customer reveals any ideas, new requirements or information about the competition which might have implications for the range of products, prices and service on offer, then the salesman can immediately go on-line and send the relevant information to the company via the information highway. Such indications of the way markets are developing can, if there are enough of them, constitute an early warning of trends, a clue as to what patterns are developing. The salesman stays with his customer during the entire after-sales period. He is the customer's problem-solver, and will still be there when he wants a new car. To back up such total devotion to the customer what is needed is: reliable information, deliveries, deadlines, services and problem-solving by a company that is responsive to its customer – a "company that breathes". In the long term, many familiar things will disappear – for example the piles of unanswered customer enquiries and complaints which, in these days of instant communications, can easily turn into a lot full of unsold cars.

A car to drive, a car to live with, to experience life through, to enhance your status with, a car that comes with a total service package, a car with a guarantee, a car that gets you there, a car that is kind to the environment, a car one can resell or recycle – all these are facets of a car's value to the customer. And all these are factors in his decision whether or not to buy. They often all add up to much more than the actual purchase price. This is the value-added potential of the "company that breathes" – the company that knows what all this is worth to the customer. You will

Winning customers through service and speed

- Responsiveness to customer wishes
- Demand-driven product range with continual updating
- 14-day delivery with 100% reliability
- Round-the-clock service and warranty
- Ongoing learning process based on customer wishes and product deficits

only "win over" your customer if you offer better value and are faster, more personal in your approach, more customer-oriented, more responsive to the customer's needs and individuality, and able to make purchasing a car into a total experience – like buying a house. Anyone wanting to harness this extra value-added first has to think in these dimensions and become aware of the customer's needs.

A breathing company like this draws heavily on the enthusiasm of its workforce. Total commitment – from order to delivery – is required from everyone, including the unions. Vis-à-vis the customer there have to be standards which every member of the workforce identifies with totally. A genuinely customer-oriented company cannot constantly have its external image tarnished for internal reasons. It may be possible to repair a particular situation with your present customer on a one-off basis, but this is offset by the greater damage to one's image and the failure to deliver the goods to potential customers. And what does a customer who has been let down care about the fragmented system of trade unions in a country, or the delivery problems you are having with company X, or the delay in developing a certain product?

Many old attitudes are no longer compatible with a breathing company – from working to rule and demarcation disputes to Saturday shut-downs...

In the markets: Innovation, Quality, Service, Speed

A "company that breathes" also has to think in terms of the customers of the future. What will their expectations be in 1999? What kinds of customer relations, regional markets and niche demand will be important then? What standards of service will be expected? The innovation cycle is no longer determined by the engineers but by the customers. Also, the product cycle also has to be demand-driven. Furthermore, it has to be possible to speed up the product cycle when demand for a particular product collapses earlier than predicted, or competitors start setting the pace. The development of modular sytems and common product platforms for the different classes of vehicle within the VW Group has already gone a long way towards responding to this need, preparing the way for body options and vehicle types which can be rapidly varied and renewed.

The overriding principle has to be total responsiveness to the customer's requirements – both external and internal customers. The breathing company must think with the customer, move with the markets on innovation, quality, speed and value for mon-

Winning customers through innovation

- Openness to other people's ideas
- Courage to experiment
- Enjoyment of the unconventional
- Desire to take on and delegate responsibility
- Inspiring customers through reliability
- Strength to change
- Entrepreneurial freedom
- Transparency and commitment

ey. It must be prepared to respond faster – and to offer more innovation, higher quality and greater reliability than its competitors.

In our experience, a company can only succeed in being more innovative and achieving total quality orientation and efficient change management if all those concerned can be persuaded to look beyond their own horizons and develop a feeling that they are playing in a world league – irrespective of the distances involved. If Volkswagen were only producing for the German market it would soon shrink into insignificance! For a global player – in terms of workforce and markets – every market is a home market.

Nowadays, we operate in a situation of total and open competition – and this means that companies are coming under increasing pressure. A "company that breathes" is one that accepts the consequences of this change from a seller's to a buyer's market. No longer do our costs and profit expectations determine prices – it is now the achievable market price which determines our costs and profit margins. The market determines even the costs and the necessary value-added element, and a company therefore has no choice but to be led by the market. This reversal of the classic approach is, in itself, a reason to undertake a thorough re-engineering of the business aimed at mobilising the full potential of value-added activities and reducing costs wherever possible. The unlimited and open competition to which companies are exposed nowadays also means an explosive growth in quality expectations. Yesterday's quality product cannot be sold today. And this constitutes another major challenge – survival of the fittest!

Winning customers through quality

- Technical quality
- Functional quality
- Aesthetic quality
- Service quality
- Rival-beating quality

Nowadays a company's traditional assets – its financial resources and technical expertise – are simply not enough. The decisive characteristic of the breathing company is the degree to which every member of the management and workforce adopts an entrepreneurial approach to everything he does.

Everyone can contribute enthusiasm and innovative ideas. Quality doesn't hurt – and change invigorates!

Goals are not something you come across by chance – you have to set them! We all have it in us to create value-added for the customer:

- Every employee is encouraged to become involved in an ongoing process of discovery, invention, development and innovation.
- Every employee can and must define, document, monitor and continually improve standards and processes.

- Every employee can and should be able to distinguish between what is important and what is irrelevant, what is a source of dynamism or paralysis, a source of motivation or frustration. Everyone must be able to tell the difference between what is challenging and constructive and what is inert and unproductive.

The key to becoming a "company that breathes" is to be imbued with this value-added spirit.

The buyer's market that we find ourselves operating in, increasingly dictates to companies the degree to which overall costs can be passed on to the customer. However, precisely how these costs are distributed across the spectrum of processes and between the company, its suppliers and the workforce, is still open – and therefore becomes the focus of improvement efforts. No process is spared scrutiny – product development, manufacturing, purchasing, marketing or human resources planning.

Pull instead of push – the breathing company

Many areas have already been scrutinised by the automotive industry – rationalisation of manufacturing processes, reduction of suppliers' prices, research and personnel costs. Now the spotlight has focused on the entire marketing process, from the receipt of orders via production right down to delivery to the customer. Few people are aware that the marketing process itself (from the manufacturer via the wholesaler and retailer to the customer) actually accounts for a considerable proportion of the final price of a vehicle. Transportation costs and capital investment in warehousing, trade margins and marketing add up to a burden of millions of Deutschmarks for a company like Volkswagen – and this has to be passed on to the customer. This is where a lot can be achieved by a breathing company. By thoroughly re-engineering processes and procedures, greater value-added can be achieved for the customer, the dealer and the company itself.

"Pull instead of push" – that is the essence of the breathing company

Instead of trying to optimise capacities and production programmes and making up for a lack of orders by producing unspecified quantities of a product – which then have to be forced on to the dealers and the markets – the manufacturing process in the factories is now exclusively determined by orders received from the dealer or the customer. The undertaking given to the custom-

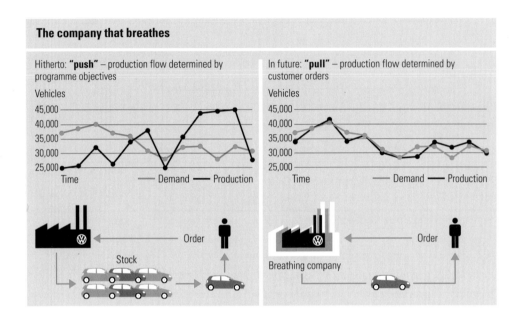

The company that breathes

Hitherto: **"push"** – production flow determined by programme objectives

In future: **"pull"** – production flow determined by customer orders

er that he will receive the vehicle chosen by the deadline required has to be translated into the entire internal chain of processes, from the acceptance of the order via scheduling, material planning, human resources deployment, production control, quality control right down to final delivery. And all those concerned must understand and be committed to the process involved.

The opportunities offered by such an approach are enormous:

• greater customer satisfaction
• enhanced customer loyalty
• increased sales potential
• reduced stock
• reduced sales incentives
• less time off the road and fewer repairs under warranty
• lower process costs
• generally improved market opportunities

A "company that breathes" requires systems that are consistent throughout, flexible capacity and human resources management – including suppliers – and a shorter flow of data and processes. It must also be clear what the critical success factors are and where bottlenecks could occur, so that an early-warning system can trigger a rapid response as required. In times of lean investment, the concept of a "company that breathes" becomes a major challenge for the manufacturer and his suppliers.

This total orientation towards the customer means a massive rethink for companies which developed in the days when manufacturers ruled the market.

Not all employees yet appreciate that every single action on their part can increase or decrease the company's business prospects and options – and every contact with the (external or internal) customer can influence whether or not the company ultimately meets that customer's requirements.

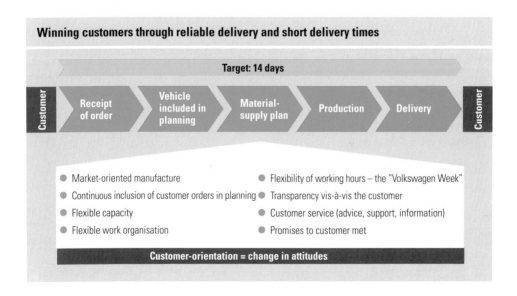

Winning customers through reliable delivery and short delivery times

Target: 14 days

Customer → Receipt of order → Vehicle included in planning → Material-supply plan → Production → Delivery → Customer

- Market-oriented manufacture
- Continuous inclusion of customer orders in planning
- Flexible capacity
- Flexible work organisation
- Flexibility of working hours – the "Volkswagen Week"
- Transparency vis-à-vis the customer
- Customer service (advice, support, information)
- Promises to customer met

Customer-orientation = change in attitudes

Experience teaches us that at least two thirds of managers have to be convinced of the necessity of a change – otherwise there is a danger that if too many drag their feet the process grinds to a halt.

Priority had to be given to fully involving management, workforce and unions in the breathing company through appropriate collective agreements. Unlike previous "management revolutions" the trade union and works council could not – and did not wish to – merely sit back passively to see what the prospect of success of this latest "fashion" was before they considered whether or not to adjust their attitudes accordingly.

The human resources systems in a breathing company

The slightest change in customer requirements and expectations must be taken seriously and responded to as rapidly as possible. The notion of a "company that breathes" is not just a fashionable slogan but rather a joint response on the part of all those who have grasped the importance of total customer-orientation. Volkswagen has already started the process of adapting its human resources systems to the needs of the breathing company. Flexible human resources availability and working hours provide the basis for an approach whereby it is the customer who determines the deployment of resources. A central element of the acceptability concept involves the decoupling of pay from performance. Instead of operating under the uncertainty of a "work on call" system, the

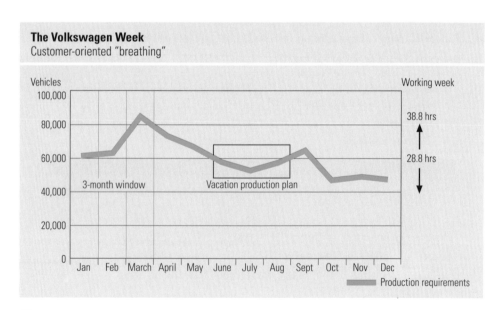

The Volkswagen Week
Customer-oriented "breathing"

employee knows in advance the guaranteed monthly salary he will receive and the maximum working hours for which he will be required.

A rolling system of three-month planning creates an additional predictability for shift-work organisation and the actual working hours of each individual. This three-month plan covers all aspects of human resources capacity and working hours. At its heart lies the concept of the Volkswagen Week – a further development of the 4-day working-week which offers the greater flexibility required by a breathing company. This can make a significant contribution towards reducing delivery times from several weeks to 14 days over the next few years.

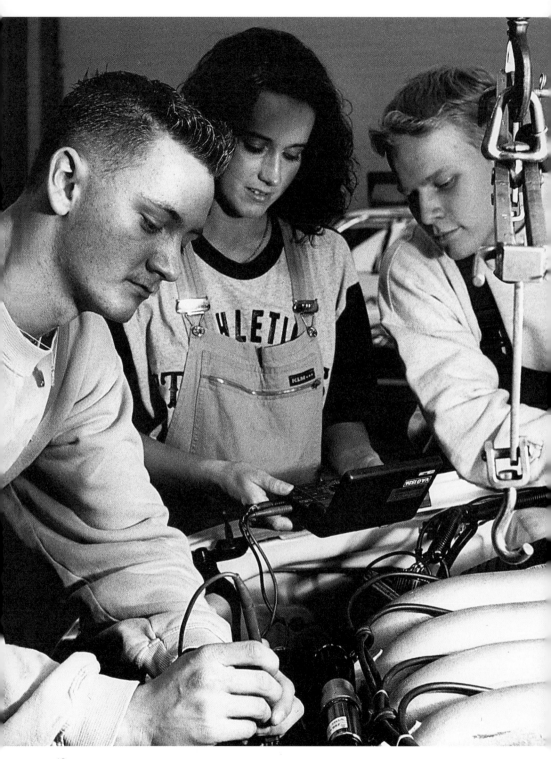

M4 – the workforce as a source of competitive advantage

"Mehrfachqualifiziert, mobil, mitgestaltend und menschlich"

It is important that the Volkswagen workforce understands what is being demanded of it. The "M4" profile (translated: multi-skilled, mobile, creative and people-oriented) is designed to provide just such orientation. How can the human resources within a breathing company be used to give that company a competitive advantage? Identification with the objectives set and full integration into the team are as important as the ability to mobilise the workforce through motivation and personal development.

Workforce and management

Competitive jobs always go hand in hand with attractive, high-quality products manufactured at reasonable cost using efficient manufacturing technology. However, nowadays the transparency of the competitive situation makes it increasingly impossible to achieve a significant technological edge over one's competitors. Every opportunity taken to upgrade a plant in a particular location or to change a product immediately offers competitors the chance to copy or compensate for the advantage gained.

The only remaining scope for competing is related to the costs of company locations. These include negotiated wage agreements and relevant legislation – all of which affect labour costs and are therefore crucial elements in determining the advantages or disadvantages of a particular location. To put it bluntly: what is at stake here is the survival of high-cost manufacturing locations. The question is: now that global sourcing and investment in lean manufacturing technology have pared down all the other costs affecting competitiveness, how can this final battle be won and our factories freed from the burden of excessive human resources costs?

M4 is an ambitious attempt by Volkswagen to use human resources to give the company a competitive edge, based on the principle that everyone's performance can be improved – through proper leadership and human resources development, and with the appropriate coaching.

One of the major challenges facing management in the future is how to compensate for the disadvantages of high-cost locations by making full use of the human resources available. It is the mark of a top company that it can derive strength, dynamism and competitive advantage from its human capital. Of course a workforce of above-average quality involves above-average costs – but nobody would regard this as a disadvantage in terms of competitiveness. A company which wishes to remain at the top therefore has to attempt to bring its employees up to a level at which they "earn their keep". Every time a decision is made regarding an individual, one needs to be aware that what is at stake is human capital with a value of over DM 1 million.

The new approach developed by Volkswagen is known by the abbreviation M4. This is based on four key adjectives in German describing the ideal workforce: "mehrfachqualifiziert, mobil, mitgestaltend und menschlich" – multi-skilled, mobile, creative and people oriented. The idea is to offer every employee a clear model of the characteristics which the company expects him to display so as to help put it on a competitive footing. It offers each member of the workforce a scale against which to measure himself and his performance, and identifies areas where complete professionalism is expected in order to preserve his job in the face of the competition. Ideally, everyone knows where he stands: within the team via objectives, targets, audits and quality-circles; and at a personal level via a multiple appraisal process which precedes every developmental step and is comparable to a form of internal customer evaluation.

This approach is based on the realisation that keen pricing and competitiveness can virtually only be achieved if the process of setting objectives, providing information and assessing areas for improvement can be transferred from management level to the more immediate level of the workforce itself. There is little point in managers returning from Japan or the USA full of enthu-

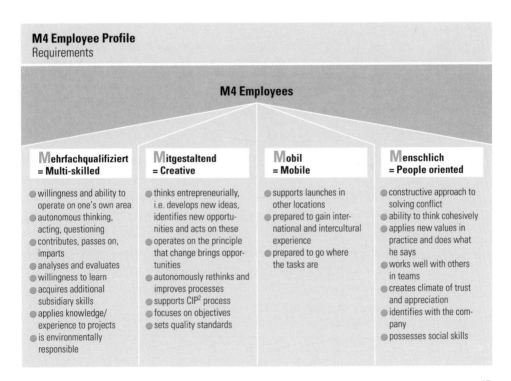

M4 Employee Profile
Requirements

M4 Employees

Mehrfachqualifiziert = **Multi-skilled**	**M**itgestaltend = **Creative**	**M**obil = **Mobile**	**M**enschlich = **People oriented**
• willingness and ability to operate on one's own area • autonomous thinking, acting, questioning • contributes, passes on, imparts • analyses and evaluates • willingness to learn • acquires additional subsidiary skills • applies knowledge/experience to projects • is environmentally responsible	• thinks entrepreneurially, i.e. develops new ideas, identifies new opportunities and acts on these • operates on the principle that change brings opportunities • autonomously rethinks and improves processes • supports CIP[2] process • focuses on objectives • sets quality standards	• supports launches in other locations • prepared to gain international and intercultural experience • prepared to go where the tasks are	• constructive approach to solving conflict • ability to think cohesively • applies new values in practice and does what he says • works well with others in teams • creates climate of trust and appreciation • identifies with the company • possesses social skills

siasm for what they have seen, if the knowledge they have acquired is not actually put into practice. In future, no job and no service will escape the process of benchmarking and benchlearning, so that all those concerned will have an opportunity to move closer to their goals and to sharpen their competitive edge.

The M4 model forms the basis of a long-term approach developed by Volkswagen, which the company has now started to implement step by step. Its aim is to use the autonomy and motivation of the workforce as an instrument for establishing and retaining a competitive advantage.

M4 makes demands on everybody. However, what does it actually mean in reality for a highly varied workforce ranging from apprentices right up to senior managers?

Multi-skilled: the M4 profile covers the entire range of skills and knowledge, from basic competence for working in the automotive industry, through the skills required for complex processes, right up to the development of new skills and leading-edge ideas.

The ability to "learn and work with and for others" is gaining importance as an element of the multi-skilling process.

What is crucial is that at every level the individual should also have competence which goes beyond his specialist skills. This includes a willingness and ability to familiarise oneself with new jobs and tasks; an ability to question one's own thinking and actions, to acquire new knowledge and pass it on to others, to recognise standards of performance and failure to reach these, to work in conjunction with others to meet the customer's requirements, and to take on specific responsibility for value-added activities. "We want to be the best" – this idea must permeate all levels of the company, from the shop floor to the boardroom. The achievement of this goal depends mainly on a team effort – without, however, denying the importance of outstanding individual effort.

Creative: the concept of participation within Volkswagen has come a long way from non-committal rights of consultation based on co-determination regulations to being a much more comprehensive idea of creative involvement.

The scope ranges from lively and critical participation in vocational training sessions, via commitment within a team, active involvement in the Continuous Improvement Process (CIP[2]) and the employee suggestion programme, to different levels of responsibility at management level and far-reaching involvement in strategic decision-making processes for the entire company at top management level. The abbreviation CIP is "squared" to indicate how quickly organisational processes had to be optimised on the "snowball" principle. Reduced hierarchies, concentration on processes rather than structures – all these trends mean that the emphasis on value-added is growing, and employees are being encouraged to take an entrepreneurial approach to their own jobs. Empowerment of the workforce means involving the employees in developing new ideas, seizing new opportunities and constantly seeking to improve processes and achieve better results and higher standards. The full potential of the workforce, regulated and controlled in the past, is now required to speed up the process of change – a change which will be most successful if the works council can share the load and become actively involved.

Mobile: working in a global company means that the Volkswagen World provides the geographical framework within which individuals can be deployed as required. The degree of mobility required obviously differs from the blue-collar worker to the one-world manager whose place of work is the entire Volkswagen world. But mobility has to become the norm for everyone – the ability to change jobs within one plant, to move from one plant to another, and to move between different countries and cultures. Wherever someone is required within the Volkswagen World, an employee can

Mobility is a prerequisite for promotion – if you want to move upwards you must be prepared to move somewhere else.

be expected to be assigned for a reasonable and defined period of time. Projects, international assignments, exchange of experience, know-how transfer, new model launch support, adjustments in personnel levels, personal career development plan, and tandem coaching – a breathing company must be able to respond to its requirements on a global basis. Anyone wishing to succeed within the company's network must not only learn to speak various company languages but also familiarise themselves with the different cultures of the company's various locations.

People oriented: finding solutions to problems can require considerable strength of character – but it is also important to be able to cope with weakness too, to take a constructive, integrative approach, offer encouragement and support and act as a role model. This positive and target-oriented behaviour ensures the success of the process.

There will always be people who react and think faster than others. The courage and determination required to push through an idea – even against considerable resistance – are further human qualities which a company has to promote.

If everyone with a bright idea first has to find somebody at top management level to promote it before there is any hope of being taken seriously, then a company is still on the wrong track. Everybody should be able to expect a sympathetic and constructive reception of new ideas. We need ideas to be promoted – not power-positions consolidated.

Everyone, from foreman to board member, must display leadership – both professionally and emotionally. A corporate culture with a human touch needs to inspire confidence and arouse enthusiasm for new ideas and objectives. If a person is to perform well, he must enjoy his job.

The concept of M4 amongst management and workforce means that hierarchies have been replaced by an internal league of skills – involving teams, centres, and different locations. The emphasis has shifted away from a person's hierarchical powers towards his actual skills and capabilities.

The challenges contained in the M4 profile for the breathing company include: total customer-orientation, management of change, concentration on value-added – i.e. being better, faster and more cost-effective than anyone else.

Introduction of the M4 approach has swept away many of the hierarchical attitudes which blocked progress and smothered motivation in the past. The key concepts are now: greater openness, benchmarking, assessment centres and multiple appraisal selection processes, team work, encouragement of centres of excellence, fostering of genuine responsibility and recognition of competence rather than formal powers and a limited outlook – and reduction of management layers within the company.

Not that it is easy to grow into this new M4 world. Too many people still rely on the "old-boy" network and think in old structures. But the changes already achieved – which are documented in this book – show how determined the company is to release new energies. M4's determination to use the workforce to gain a new edge over competitors has left its mark on every aspect of human resources. Volkswagen has achieved a radical break with the past with its new approach to working hours – a complete paradigm change from mere presence at work to direct involvement in processes and consultation over goals and objectives, and a common wage policy with agreed performance criteria for blue- and white-collar workers alike.

Teamwork

"Teamwork is everything" is one of the essential principles we have applied in order to focus efforts and improve results. Over the past few years, the introduction of group work, CIP[2], ideas management, and new organisational and management structures have given rise to an unexpected number of different approaches and models.

The M4 motto: "Do it!" encourages individuals to think for themselves. The result has been hundreds of proposals for improvements – all of them with the advantage that from the very outset they have the backing of those who thought them up in the first place. However, this can only be permitted during the initial phase – if left to their own devices, formal groups have a tendency to develop a life of their own and lose direction. Furthermore, a situation can often occur whereby a lack of patience or an initially negative reaction on the part of management can result in both parties – managers and workforce representatives – returning to the teams with differing signals, leaving the workers themselves uncertain as to whose opinion is right. Furthermore, the top performers of the European automotive industry still largely run plants with classic working structures, whereas towards the lower end there are a considerable number with comprehensive group work programmes.

Thus – despite occasional impressions to the contrary – work groups have yet to be introduced across the board in most factories in the European automotive industry. However, unless companies have the courage to introduce more efficient ways of using their human resources in the form of teamwork, there is a danger of a backlash resurgence of the specialist in an attempt to enhance competitiveness.

That is why it is all the more crucial for management – and the entire organisation – to support the advantages of teamwork:

- a self-directed team which aims at achieving goals which it is able to determine and influence itself
- to subject the team to benchmarking of performance objectives and to make it responsible for implementation
- to deploy the team in clearly defined areas of work where it has a chance of achieving verifiable success in a joint effort
- to link further training and job rotation within the team with fulfilment of the relevant standards
- to unleash the team's full potential through the use of coordinators, ongoing discussion, CIP[2] workshops, flexible human resources deployment and the setting of productivity goals
- to give the team an opportunity to achieve rationalisation goals by making full use of their capacity, even getting involved in indirect activities instead of facing dismissal

Experience has taught us that, in addition to these elements, to be effective the approach also requires a determination not to avoid difficult problems but to tackle them head on.

For the team approach to be successful, the selection and quality of the team spokesperson has to be right. Selection by the team itself does not in all cases automatically mean that the most appropriate person is chosen. If there is clear disagreement, then the selection process and provisions for the lodging of objections must operate effectively.

When negotiating on performance, it is important to move away from the old, Taylorist idea of a standard wage and standard performance. A competition-oriented approach to performance has to be found which goes beyond methods-time measurement and other ways of assessing work. Volkswagen has succeeded in signing collective agreements which achieve this step towards a dynamic appraisal of personnel performance linked with new wage structures.

Moving around on assembly lines, unnecessary personnel upheavals, allowing quality defects to slip through and be remedied at a later stage, losing unit-production as a result of poor group dynamics, failure to use recovery time and interruptions to carry out other tasks – there are many things which need to be discussed and remedied at plant level. On the other hand, the plant layout should be conducive to operating in teams, enabling them to be in visual contact with each other, and ensuring a clear allocation of responsibilities. Thus, for example, interfaces with purchase parts need to be set up, quality and materials management procedures for component suppliers prior to installation have to be incorporated, and the group has to be allowed to rectify faults through its own efforts without halting the production flow.

One way of speeding up team work is the modular approach to plant design. The entire process chain is divided into production units, in which modules are manufactured largely independently of each other. Various different approaches are being tried out in the automotive industry. Up to 100 production units are defined, and these integrate all functions (manufacturing, maintenance, quality assurance, logistics, development and planning). They are thus in a position to ensure that the customer further along the chain only receives the highest quality.

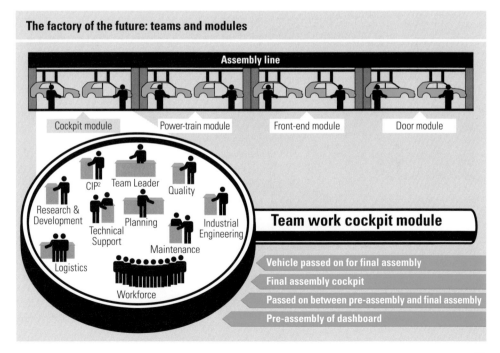

The factory of the future: teams and modules

Assembly line

Cockpit module   Power-train module   Front-end module   Door module

CIP²   Team Leader

Quality

Research & Development

Planning

Technical Support

Industrial Engineering

Maintenance

Logistics

Workforce

Team work cockpit module

Vehicle passed on for final assembly

Final assembly cockpit

Passed on between pre-assembly and final assembly

Pre-assembly of dashboard

This approach thus goes further than the use of individual working groups and makes teamworking into the central principle for organisation and management of all processes in a plant. Modules can be entire division like the paint-shop, but can also be a specific assembly unit, such as the cockpit. What is important is a comprehensive approach to organisation of tasks and decentralisation of responsibility up to the moment when the module is ready for inclusion in the vehicle or for passing on to the next process. Internal and external suppliers can be incorporated into this "team factory" and can take on responsibility for a module.

A new age of modular production has dawned for Volkswagen on a global basis. This means that the introduction of team work right across the board in all its manufacturing locations is essential. It has already reached an understanding with workforce representatives in Europe that they will support this strategy. Where modularisation involves the incorporation of external suppliers right down to the assembly line, workforce representatives are involved, so as to ensure that the sensibilities of various groups of employees under the same roof are catered for. Modular production will be one of the last major opportunities to achieve significant increases in productivity via a

The modular factory helps create an ideal organisational environment for teamwork.

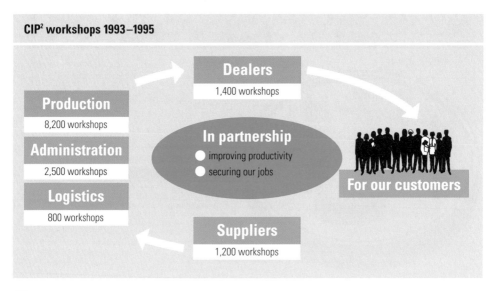

CIP² workshops 1993–1995

Production
8,200 workshops

Administration
2,500 workshops

Logistics
800 workshops

Dealers
1,400 workshops

In partnership
● improving productivity
● securing our jobs

Suppliers
1,200 workshops

For our customers

team approach. It is therefore all the more important to gather experience with this approach and concentrate globally on those variants which are most successful. The ground was prepared by Volkswagen with the world-wide organisation of 14,000 CIP² workshops since 1993. Workshops are held by employees and moderators according to an established pattern. Over a period of a week, they work on developing measures for improving performance and quality in specific product or problem areas. Measures for improving working conditions and environmental protection are also regularly defined. The results of the workshop are assessed financially and, where possible, implemented immediately.

Since the programme was first launched, some 86,000 measures have been defined by CIP² teams, of which some 64,000 have been implemented. Teams in all Volkswagen manufacturing locations from Wolfsburg to Shanghai, Sao Paolo to Mladá Boleslav have been involved. CIP² workshops are also held in the administration areas, for suppliers and dealer organisations, in a bid to bring an overall improvement to the process chains and value-added. In addition to quality and productivity, areas requiring attention include reductions in material in process and lead-time as well as complexity and production area.

Idea management at Volkswagen

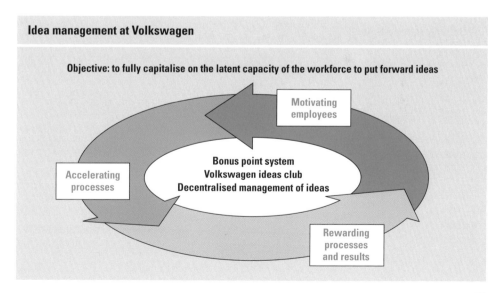

Objective: to fully capitalise on the latent capacity of the workforce to put forward ideas

Motivating employees

Accelerating processes

Bonus point system
Volkswagen ideas club
Decentralised management of ideas

Rewarding processes and results

Operating in tandem with the employee suggestion programme and other programmes for increasing workforce motivation, CIP^2 offers teams a powerful instrument for enhancing competitiveness. Every young management trainee now has a period as a CIP^2 moderator incorporated into his development plan – and this offers a valuable source of experience. The immediate superior is set to play an increasingly important role in "idea management", and decisions made at local level on suggestions and CIP^2 results can accelerate the process. This is more important than lengthy and complex appraisal procedures carried out in an attempt to achieve the ultimate in thoroughness and fairness.

Idea management means using the creativity of the workforce as a strategic factor in improving competitiveness. The aims are:

- to fully exploit the ideas put forward by members of the workforce
- to reward ideas
- to link incentives for involvement in CIP^2 and suggestions for improvements
- to provide more scope for immediate superiors to implement the ideas of their subordinates more rapidly
- to enhance the economic effects

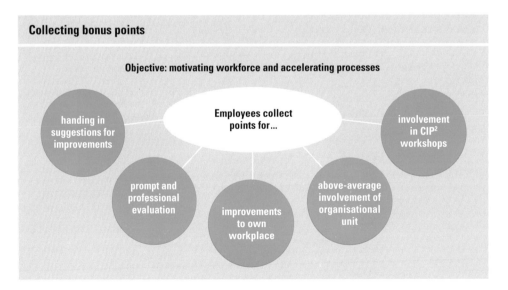

Collecting bonus points

Objective: motivating workforce and accelerating processes

Employees collect points for...

handing in suggestions for improvements

involvement in CIP^2 workshops

prompt and professional evaluation

improvements to own workplace

above-average involvement of organisational unit

Like other companies, Volkswagen would benefit from a further boost to ideas management. The existing system is a decentralised one: local management directly implements ideas and suggested improvements within their area of responsibility and directly rewards the members of the workforce involved. A system of bonus points encourages workforce involvement and rewards results. In future employees will collect bonus points for:

- handing in suggestions for improvements
- achieving tangible improvements in their own field of work
- prompt and professional evaluation and feedback
- above-average involvement of their own organisational unit
- participation in a CIP[2] workshop and the resulting measures

The idea is to foster a spirit of competition amongst employees. Volkswagen offers it own prizes and incentives – ranging from safety training, and test drives with new models to sponsored events and travel within the Volkswagen World.

An ongoing process of improvement is standard practice in the company: this small step for each employee would mean a massive leap for Volkswagen and its competitiveness.

Integration and differentiation

The more directly an individual and his personal motivation can be addressed, the easier it is to inspire commitment. Where individuals work in large organisations there is always a danger that motivation and enthusiasm will begin to fade into anonymity.

Where there is a large workforce, there is only too often a silent, passive majority. Comparative studies by corporate consultants indicate that the less successful companies tend to have a large workforce, most of which operates virtually invisibly. In a large company such people can easily become a hindrance to progress. Often nobody is unhappier about the situation than those involved – many of whom in their private lives may be actively involved in local politics or in running clubs, and yet clock in for work day after day without ever being allowed to make decisions about expenditure of a mere DM 100.

If structures could be opened up, individuals given greater responsibility and freedom, and more team spirit and localised decision-making introduced, then this would be a revolutionary step towards a new future.

The effect on many people of these trends can be a feeling of uncertainty and confusion. No longer can they simply turn up for work and carry out the tasks according to their job description and employment contract. More is being demanded of them – as a demonstration of commitment and their contribution to retaining the competitiveness of the company, they are expected to produce results, create quality, reduce costs, introduce improvements. No longer are they tiny cogs in some massive, anonymous machine – they can now play a direct role in keeping the main wheels turning.

If this direct appeal to people's personal motivation is to succeed, then sensitivity towards their professional and personal situation is required. What makes an individual tick, what is the driving force within the group, the social environment? In addition to having much in common, every group within the workforce also has its particular interests – young and old, men and women, Germans and foreigners. The working atmosphere at Volkswagen is made up of groupings like these – with 9,000, 16,000, 20,000, 40,000 members – all with their particular generational attitudes and feelings. A company, for example, that does not take the younger generation seriously cannot expect them to display full motivation in return. Therefore, one that allows parts of its workforce to be marginalised ends up not only with a poor working atmosphere but also with poor performance figures.

Promotion of women in the workplace

Proper integration combined with appropriate differentiation of the workforce is by no means a passé concept. Democratisation and integration of society requires, amongst other things, equal access by all groups within that society to the opportunities on offer.

Since the late 1980s, Volkswagen's human resources policy has focused on promoting women in the workplace. The company has been concerned to make it clear to women that what used to be a typically "male" world now confidently expects and recognises that they can make a full contribution at all levels.

An example of this policy of equality is the special pro-gramme launched to promote women in the workplace. It is aimed at all groups of women within Volkswagen:

- from apprentices
- semi-skilled press-shop workers
- skilled workers
- office workers
- women returning to work
- to women in specialist and management positions

The programme focuses on working with these women to develop ideas which can contribute towards their achieving equality.

A combination of special careers advice sessions aimed ex-clusively at young women – including introductory courses and special "technology days", special seminars for schoolgirls, and in-service training courses for teachers has resulted in the pro-portion of female applicants being offered apprenticeships in commercial/technical areas growing from 30% to 45% since 1991. Every year, the number of skilled female workers grows by 10%, and Volkswagen now leads the automotive industry in this respect, with over 15% women in technical jobs. Other elements in the programme include projects for training female production

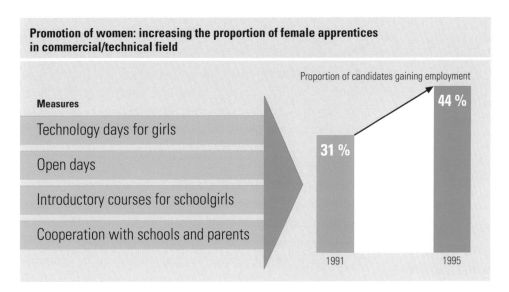

Promotion of women: increasing the proportion of female apprentices in commercial/technical field

Proportion of candidates gaining employment

Measures

Technology days for girls

Open days

Introductory courses for schoolgirls

Cooperation with schools and parents

31 %

44 %

1991

1995

supervisors and programmes for recruiting women as engineers and international young management trainees. Women now account for an impressive 30% of those on the international trainee programme, with its largely technical bias.

Even though the present 3% share which women have of senior management jobs is not so impressive, the proportion of newly-appointed managers who are female is growing considerably. We have a vision of a future in which the proportion of female management staff will reflect that of the management replacement candidate pool, at 30%. To achieve this, much will have to be done in the way of removing barriers to promotion – and Volkswagen has already developed and approved the appropriate models. VW families include almost 65,000 children and youngsters under the age of 18. Half of these are below the age of ten and therefore require particular care and supervision. Today's working time arrangements allow scope for looking after the family to a degree unimaginable in the past; 58% of women (compared with 47% of men) have declared themselves completely satisfied with the 4-day week. The crucial advantage they perceive is that it allows them more time for their family.

An additional advantage offered is the possibility of up to 5 years' leave of absence with guaranteed reintegration. This can be combined with the statutory paid leave to which new parents are entitled. To ensure that women have the necessary skills to be able to return to work, they can also attend special workshops with child-care facilities. Volkswagen is developing and implementing a model for company-supported child care, for example in conjunction with local authorities. By consulting with local women's networks, the company is trying to help make promotion of women an integral part of regional economic and structural policy.

From apprentice to fully-fledged member of the workforce

Integration and support for young people within the company is not simply a matter of offering them a full-time appointment. A recent Volkswagen study entitled "Targeting Young People" looked at what motivates young people to apply for jobs in the company and what their initial experiences are. For almost 100% of those surveyed, Volkswagen was more than just an average employer. The initial motivation for applying to the company was related to material aspects rather than career considerations. Career and training opportunities were ranked sixth, after salary, social benefits, security, size of company and guarantee of employment after training.

The young people continued to have this attitude even after they had been given a full-time job. More than two thirds of them claimed to be satisfied with the trade or profession they had been trained in, and almost 90% wished to make a career within the company, but 70% complained of the lack of professional motivation of the "others". Even though the survey is now somewhat dated, the results underline one important point: it would be a serious mistake if company policy underestimated the effect which such attitudes amongst young people can have on the working atmosphere in the future. For many young people, the transition to the world of work is a shock which has to be overcome before they can develop M4 qualities. More personal care and supervision can help overcome the anonymity of the company.

It would be fatal for a company like Volkswagen, which sails so close to the competitive wind and relies to such a great extent on the skills of everyone on board, if young people were to feel that they were not important for its long-term future.

Volkswagen intends to take closer care of its youngsters. In future, regular contacts and discussions will form part of the process, from the initial appointment of apprentices to their final integration into full employment. By tightening up and improving selection procedures, the company will be in a position to recognise potential for development from the very outset and avoid expensive mistakes. The selection criteria are based on the requirements and subject-matter of the various trades and also on the requirements of the company as a whole.

The selection process is intended to ensure that, from the range of places available, applicants are offered the apprenticeship which best matches their inclinations and abilities. The rigorous standards applied in each manufacturing location are based on the training results achieved by the Volkswagen Coaching Company (Volkswagen Coaching Gesellschaft) and the standards of competitors. Standards and selection criteria are subject-

Appointment of apprentices

7 steps to apprenticeship contract

Selection Committee

Medical examination

Structured interview

Induction and aptitude test

Qualitative assessment according to pre-selection criteria

Formally correct application received by deadline

Information sessions for school leavers and personnel marketing

ed to a thorough review on a yearly basis to ensure that the recruitment process is continuously being improved.

The applicants most suited to the particular plant concerned are identified within the various types of school. An appropriate recruitment scheme is then set up which takes into account the situation of the plant and local requirements. In addition to school qualifications and an aptitude for particular subjects, the new procedure also takes into account abilities and interests outside the specialist field.

The first step in the six-stage process of selection is for the applicant to submit a formal application by the deadline set. Applications are then evaluated in terms of school-leaving grades, taking into account the pre-selection criteria related to the particular plant and the requirements of the trade or profession concerned. The next step involves providing candidates with information about the requirements and criteria of vocational training at Volkswagen and an aptitude test in order to help them make their choice – and to determine their suitability.

Those candidates who display the necessary aptitude are then invited to a structured interview with specially trained staff who compare the individual's abilities with the requirements of the trade or profession concerned. Objectivity is guaranteed by the highly structured nature of the interview, but the direct personal contact ensures that the individual nature of each applicant may be expressed. If it is found that the candidate's abilities and potential – interest in an apprenticeship at Volkswagen, ability to cope with problems, willingness to work with others, communication skills – meet requirements, the next step is a medical examination by the company doctor.

The sixth and final step involves a selection committee, consisting of equal numbers of management and workers' representatives. This considers all the results of the selection process so far and decides whether a training contract should be offered to the candidate.

This selection process forms the basis for the total development and promotion of young people during training and beyond. In view of their youth, the emphasis is on assessing potential rather than testing existing skills. The aim is to help unsuitable applicants avoid frustration at a later stage.

The training period focuses on developing and promoting apprentices in both specialist and general interpersonal skills. During the entire training process, there is an ongoing dialogue between all those concerned on all major aspects of training.

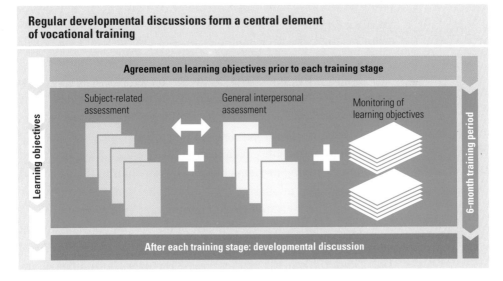

Regular developmental discussions form a central element of vocational training

Agreement on learning objectives prior to each training stage

Learning objectives

Subject-related assessment

General interpersonal assessment

Monitoring of learning objectives

6-month training period

After each training stage: developmental discussion

Regular checks on learning objectives and discussion with individuals help identify and solve problems in motivation or integration, so that as many apprentices as possible can be offered posts as skilled blue- or white-collar workers according to the M4 profile. The range of courses and facilities is impressive: basic function-related courses, supervised self-study and group-learning, practical experience parallel to theoretical courses, technology centres, creativity development, as well as motivation and leisure-time programmes. The training aims to develop a high degree of suitability for working in the automotive industry and provide apprentices with all the basic virtues of a truly customer-oriented car-maker, so that they can strengthen the team they finally join.

The process of winning over the customer starts with promising young employees having the feeling: "we're not the weakest link in the company - in fact, we're increasingly where its future lies!"

To support this close care and supervision of apprentices a plant agreement entitled "Appointment, Development and Promotion of Apprentices" has been drawn up, which sets new standards for the training process and will come into force in 1996.

Such a change was particularly necessary as Volkswagen – despite a sharp decline in its human resources requirements – is determined to maintain a policy of training beyond requirements, and integration into full-time posts. Recruitment levels are the same as in 1980, when – in those areas where Volkswagen has its plants – there were 20% more school-leavers than in 1994/5. Despite an increase in school-leavers over the last two years, the high level of applications of the 1980s has not been repeated.

Despite the fact that, in the areas in which Volkswagen plants are located, 10% of all unemployed are young people, there has not been any increase in the number of applications. This is largely because there has been a general decline in interest in typical automotive jobs, even though the chances of being offered a job after training are considerably higher than in the past. And the commitment to offering full-time employment following training means that recruitment of apprentices at Volkswagen brings a long-term commitment on the part of the company to the tune of over a million Deutschmarks – in addition to the training costs of DM 150,000. Over the last ten years, the average number of apprentices on Volkswagen's books at any one time was some 4,000 – though the figure varied. Recommending the next step in the careers of these young people requires skill and careful preparation.

From skilled worker to production supervisor

Every year, almost 1,000 skilled workers with qualifications specific to the automotive industry join the company – almost twice as many as find themselves in the final years before retirement. Thus the proportion of "skilled Volkswagen workers" is constantly growing, and today accounts for 39% of the workforce – and 51% of those employed in manufacturing. This trend reflects a general increase in levels of qualification amongst the workforce. The number of employees with university-level qualifications, especially in technical subjects, has reached a record level of 29% in the white-collar sector. This growing base of people with relevant qualifications facilitates the process of life-long learning and the development of a multi-skilled, highly adaptable workforce.

Skilled workers have the opportunity to develop their skills further and take on a broad range of responsibilities as M4 production supervisor. As well as being responsible for costs, quality, productivity, reliability of delivery and leadership in several pro-

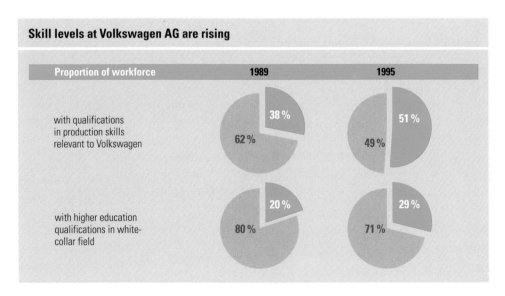

Skill levels at Volkswagen AG are rising

Proportion of workforce	1989	1995
with qualifications in production skills relevant to Volkswagen	38% / 62%	51% / 49%
with higher education qualifications in white-collar field	20% / 80%	29% / 71%

duction groups, production supervisors are increasingly also required to develop motivational, supervisory and delegating skills within the team. In the processes for which they are responsible they are expected to provide living examples of an approach epitomised by the statement: "Everyone is a customer – everyone is a supplier". Thus a good production supervisor acts both as an example to others and as an indispensable member of the team.

In order to respond to the greater emphasis on processes and teamwork, the production supervisor programme has been restructured. Gone are the foremen, and in their place there are now smaller units, which are intended to strengthen the supervisor in his role. An appropriate scheme has also been set up for selection and development of new production supervisors. Systematic pre-selection, appraisal and a personal development plan serve to provide a picture of an individual's strengths and weaknesses in terms of the M4 profile and permit appropriate individualised preparation for the tasks involved. Unlike the assessment centre for young management replacement candidates, the as-

The route to becoming an M4 production supervisor

Appointment

Observer and experienced production supervisors as coaches

Appropriate on-the-job personnel development, e.g. participation in CIP^2 workshops and throughout the process chain

Practically oriented production supervisor training/comprehensive programme of seminars

Personal Development Plan

Assessment to analyse individual strengths/weaknesses

Systematic preselection from candidates with Chamber of Industry and Commerce-supervisor qualifications or similar

sessment for production supervisors is designed not so much to provide a recommendation for future career steps as to give detailed feedback on an individual's state of knowledge and recommendations on any further training measures which are necessary.

The criteria used were based partly on surveys conducted amongst plant management and also works council members, which were then distilled into 15 core criteria in workshops, attended by male and female production supervisors. These were then incorporated in a 4-stage programme entitled "The route to becoming a production supervisor". This programme has already been tried and tested in a total of 45 assessments. Once the assessment process has been successfully completed and an individual has been confirmed as a trainee production supervisor, he is subjected to 500 hours of preparation in mainly general/interpersonal skills and systematic on-the-job training.

Skilful team leadership involves persuading members to work enthusiastically towards a common goal.

From talented employee to manager

The development programme for production supervisors displays many of the basic characteristics of Volkswagen's overall approach to management: careful selection, assessment centre, and individual development measures.

Just as the number of qualified skilled workers has increased, so, too, has the number of new employees entering the company with higher education qualifications. In the early 1980s there were only 3,000 graduates employed in the company, whereas today – despite downsizing of the workforce – the number is twice that. Here, too, an analysis of age structures reveals that more than 50% of the company's potential is to be found amongst the under-forties.

Despite an otherwise limited recruitment policy, the company has consistently managed to recruit international trainees with above-average records, international work or study experience, and high personal potential. After 15 to 18 months of "learning by doing" in various divisions and also abroad, these individuals are

Assessment Centre: criteria to achieve a recommendation for management level

Intellectual qualities	Motivation/driving force	People skills
Ability to solve problems	**Commitment to company**	**Ability to communicate/make contact**
• "Helicopter" capability	• Willingness to learn	• Extroversion
• Creative thinking	• Initiative	• Psychological sensitivity
• Decision-making behaviour	• Challenge	• Ability to listen and ask questions
• Organisational ability	• Desire to bring about change	• Verbal behaviour
	• Eagerness to perform	
	Self-confidence	**Cooperative behaviour**
	• Assessment of own competence	• Ability to work in a team
	• Willingness to take risks	• Ability to cope with conflict
	• High stress tolerance	
		Ability to convince/determination

given their first deployment within the company. Later, after the initial development stages and probationary periods are over, the very best enter the management trainee programme. Once again, the M4 profile is refined, with general intellectual ability, entrepreneurial commitment and interpersonal skills being monitored and assessed. Six experienced, specially trained VW managers evaluate the potential of ten candidates. This VW assessment lasts for three days, and ends with a recommendation as to the candidate's basic suitability to join the ranks of management. The training programmes to which the individual then proceeds concentrate on systematic training and preparation for management tasks, accompanied by job-rotation and foreign assignments.

From manager to top manager

The approach to management became increasingly based on a hierarchy of decision-making authority. Highly differentiated models with many different management levels were no longer appropriate for the new Volkswagen World, and in 1994 the company took appropriate action and reduced the system to two levels only: management and top management.

The top management levels cover individuals with wide-ranging responsibilities and important functions in VW companies, who undertake strategic tasks necessary for the further development of the company. Those who are also responsible for steering the entire Group and have international responsibilities in companies within the Group are regarded as occupying "key positions". All top managers are personally known and have the confidence of the Group Board members. Thus the Group and the Volkswagen brand are managed on a personal – rather than an anonymous – basis.

This restructuring and redefinition of management also reflects the growing importance of employees to whom the collective bargaining pay scale does not apply. These "non-tariff" or NT employees are classified within the management level at a time when non-hierarchical teams and innovative projects require nothing more than the relevant competence. Using the tried-and-tested procedure of the assessment centre, a uniform process which embraces even NT employees now offers access to the higher levels of management. Whether or not an individual takes on a specialist or management role is now largely a question of emphasis rather than being a final, irreversible decision. In any case, the candidates put forward are usually young and have only just moved into the upper salary bracket, so that their potential still has time to emerge over a longer period of monitoring. Before

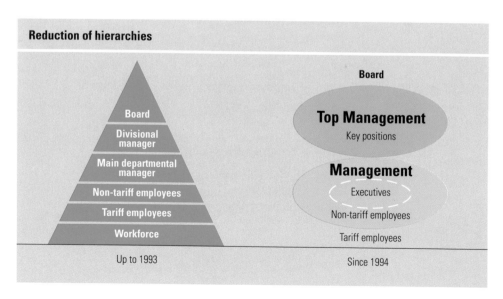

Reduction of hierarchies

Up to 1993

Board
Divisional manager
Main departmental manager
Non-tariff employees
Tariff employees
Workforce

Since 1994

Board
Top Management
Key positions
Management
Executives
Non-tariff employees
Tariff employees

they join the ranks of management, so-called 360° audits of the tasks they have completed are carried out: how is the potential manager viewed by his superiors (not his immediate supervisor) and the workforce, by customers and colleagues? The reference persons for this audit must also have an appropriate aptitude profile – in other words they must be top performers with no direct connection with the subject of the audit, must enjoy the trust of the Board and must be able to prove that they have experience of working with the candidate. Each candidate requires at least three referees from different divisions or companies within the Group.

The candidate must also be a nominated "management replacement candidate", i.e. have received a positive result at the assessment centre, and then must also be able to furnish proof of having taken part in job rotations and development seminars. Furthermore, the individual concerned must have gained international experience and have acted as a CIP[2] moderator as well as furnishing other proof of his commitment. This could include participation in the Group Junior Development Programme, with specific involvement in Group projects and networks.

Multiple assessment – the only way to management positions

Application

| Structural requirements | Human resources and Management | Personal requirements |

Multiple assessment principle
- Assessment Centres
- 3-5 referees
- now also colleagues and subordinates

Decision by the Board

The further development and preparation of individuals for top management functions – the "top 250 in the Group" – is less spectacular than many people might imagine. The emphasis here is on outstanding intellectual abilities and specialist skills over a long period of service in all parts of the Group or in other companies, as well as a high degree of business dynamism and a willingness to deliver results. If someone is going to be constantly making decisions which are crucial to the future of the company, he requires the absolute confidence of the Group Board. Furthermore, the person concerned must be able to carry others with them and achieve the changes which are so vital for the company's survival. Here, too, the multi-appraisal principle forms the basis for nominations.

What the Board is looking for is a direct link to its management team. This direct link can sometimes be taken in a literal sense – much information and many messages can be transmitted by internal electronic mail. This allows various groups to be addressed specifically – e.g. all owners of an e-mail connection, particular employees on assignment abroad, all members of the management, or only top managers. This allows the Board to pass on specific information from its most recent meetings or to state its position on topics of public interest which are being discussed in the media. This method can be used simply to send a New Year greeting to colleagues or to address them personally on other occasions – as well as officially announcing human resources or organisational changes in the company and the Group. Of course, this method of communication does not replace direct contact, but rather offers a sensible and efficient way of complementing it.

In addition to many different company bodies for steering decision-making processes in general and strategic ones in particular, the Board uses regular management meetings as an opportunity to make its views known. In addition to the usual contributions from the floor, the company also makes use of the "option-finder" – an electronic system which allows anonymous voting to take place. The "option-finder" helps create a relaxed atmosphere in which spontaneous dialogue can take place. An "option-finder" survey revealed, for example, that 33% of Volkswagen managers regarded the degree of success in restructuring in recent years as "high" or "very high", 50% regarded it as "average", and 16% as "too low". The Board uses this method to encourage direct feedback on many questions and recommendations – the managers' appraisal of Board performance, the degree of acceptance of a wage and bonus settlement, or their assessment of restructuring processes or new product segments.

This redefinition of management also constituted a challenge to the traditional bodies for co-determination and participation in management decisions. For many years the interests of management at Volkswagen have been represented by the Management Association, whether those concerned were executive employees or not. At the same time, it is fully accepted that the works council shares responsibility for all non-executive managerial employees.

The company, works council and Management Association agreed some years ago to form a "round table" at which all aspects of human resources policy for management (executive, non-executive, NT personnel) are jointly discussed. This has proved to be a successful alternative to the statutory representative committee for executive employees at Volkswagen. The works council and the association thus take on joint responsibility for representing the interests of the entire management – which goes well beyond the German statutory requirements.

Agreement on development: the Personal Development Plan

Behind all the instruments of the M4 profile, the selection procedure, the multi-appraisal principle, the 360° audit, and the various development measures and programmes is a single insight: no matter how good you are, you can always be better.

Another new idea is the Personal Development Plan, which constitutes a summary of the progress made and the agreements reached between the employee and the company. What is new here is the fact that this is not a confidential document, or an entry in some database, but rather is a document held by the employee in which the company records his appraisal and underlines the importance of developmental stages. The Personal Development Plan is a sort of passport which the M4 Employee carries on his journey through the Volkswagen World – a pocketbook sized personal document which records all the important data on a person's career – qualifications, degree of mobility, income development, and promotional measures – are all recorded at the wish of the individual. The company requires no further information and commitments (except those necessary for meeting statutory and other requirements). Thus, the time may well come

when this document is the only form of personnel record required by the independent employee of the future. The employees would then be able to use it as the basis for regular talks with supervisors.

Discussion of the Personal Development Plan is destined to form a regular part of the new approach to human resources management at local level – especially for employees to whom special promotion measures apply, or who face changes in their careers at Volkswagen. A combination of support measures at work, pilot projects involving seven groups of employees, and the deployment of local personnel officers as moderators helped to ensure that this new measure – which is part of the change from administration of people's careers to co-determination by the individual – was carefully introduced.

The success of the Personal Development Plan, depends to a large extent on the quality of the dialogue with the employee's immediate superior. Thus, the local personnel management must not leave him in the lurch. Any commitments which go beyond his immediate field of responsibility must be moderated, discussed and confirmed by the personnel manager and supported by his Division and the works council.

The Personal Development Plan is like a compass which provides orientation in the race to use human resources to create a competitive advantage.

In addition to personal control of working hours, the team approach, the notion of CIP[2], and the reduction of hierarchies, the importance of the Personal Development Plan for employee autonomy should not be underestimated. It constitutes an effective tool for the person concerned to participate in planning his development, rather than just being an anonymous member of the workforce. It is, of course, entirely up to the individual whether he wishes to have a Personal Development Plan, but it is intended to be an aid to aligning company requirements and personal wishes. The "passport" should also offer a guarantee which makes it easier for the M4 Employee to abandon established routines and experiment with greater mobility, block working hours, progressive reductions of working hours and other reasonable innovations. In principle, the Personal Development Plan can be applied to all workforce groups.

The basis for M4 human resources activities at plant level
Personnel Service Centre and Manpower Allocation Centre

The concept of the M4 Employee requires a type of supervision which no longer differentiates between white- and blue-collar workers. Such locally-based, "one-stop" supervision is provided by the Personnel Service Centre, whose role is to provide a comprehensive service covering consultation, service, information and support. This "customer-oriented" personnel service is the result of close collaboration between members of management and representatives of the workforce. The centres are organised on a decentralised basis, and offer, for all human resources issues contact persons who can offer competent advice, and a rapid, direct and confidential service. One of its more important functions is in conjunction with the newly-established Manpower Allocation Centre to ensure the availability of suitably qualified mobile personnel at the right time and in the right quantity.

Rapid changes in productivity and internal structures have created a need for a new approach to manpower assignment. The newly created Manpower Allocation Centre are intended to function as an internal link between the plants and cost centres. A satellite operation is set up in each plant and forms an integral part of personnel operations in that plant. Central coordination and control is carried out by Manpower Allocation Centre in Wolfsburg.

A special cost centre with its own budget has been set up for Manpower Allocation Centre – enabling personnel surpluses to be transferred to it if and when they are identified. This makes it easy to recognise where such surpluses exist and the personnel department can then intervene to redeploy them in an appropriate way, covering costs and adding further value in the process.

In future one of the new tasks of the human resources manager in VW plants will be that of managing mobility and person-

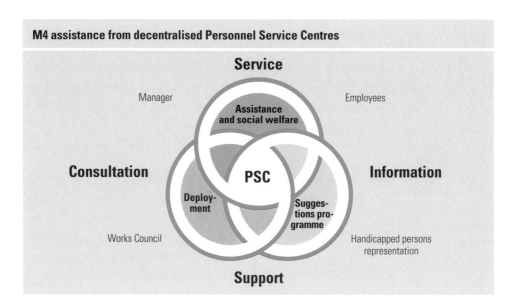

M4 assistance from decentralised Personnel Service Centres

Service

Manager   Employees

Assistance and social welfare

Consultation   PSC   Information

Deploy-ment   Sugges-tions pro-gramme

Works Council   Handicapped persons representation

Support

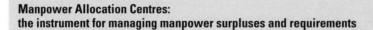

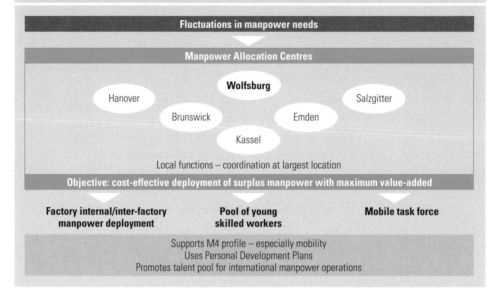

**Manpower Allocation Centres:
the instrument for managing manpower surpluses and requirements**

Fluctuations in manpower needs

Manpower Allocation Centres

Wolfsburg

Hanover

Salzgitter

Brunswick

Emden

Kassel

Local functions – coordination at largest location

Objective: cost-effective deployment of surplus manpower with maximum value-added

**Factory internal/inter-factory
manpower deployment**

**Pool of young
skilled workers**

Mobile task force

Supports M4 profile – especially mobility
Uses Personal Development Plans
Promotes talent pool for international manpower operations

nel surpluses. He will have a number of instruments at his disposal: personnel brokerage, a pool of young skilled workers, mobile project groups for international support operations, and integration of qualified staff into insourcing projects and newly-founded businesses.

In the long term, the Manpower Allocation Centre will also take on new staff and offer them an orientation phase. Its role is closely linked to a new approach to jobs and is intended to facilitate restructuring, by allowing employees not only to remain in the company during transitional periods but also to gain a useful insight into other areas of the company's operations.

Commitment to work, health and the environment

For the workforce to remain competitive, it must retain its vigour and its commitment to better working and environmental conditions. Health, safety and environmental protection must always be a central focus of corporate policy – not least in order to avoid undesirable developments. There is now a wide degree of consen-

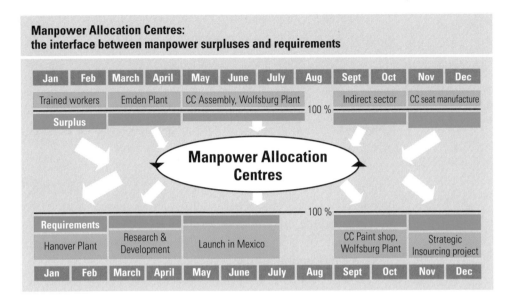

Manpower Allocation Centres:
the interface between manpower surpluses and requirements

Jan	Feb	March	April	May	June	July	Aug	Sept	Oct	Nov	Dec

Trained workers — Emden Plant — CC Assembly, Wolfsburg Plant — 100 % — Indirect sector — CC seat manufacture

Surplus

Manpower Allocation Centres

100 %

Requirements

Hanover Plant — Research & Development — Launch in Mexico — CC Paint shop, Wolfsburg Plant — Strategic Insourcing project

Jan	Feb	March	April	May	June	July	Aug	Sept	Oct	Nov	Dec

sus on objectives in this field – and on the measures necessary to achieve them. The ultimate goal is to promote the health of the workforce, humanise the workplace, and care for the environment.

In recent years there has been a radical change in the framework within which health and safety at work operates: changes in the demands made by workers, higher expectations with regard to jobs, changed patterns of illness, new production techniques. In addition to this, ongoing improvements in safety at work and the general upgrading of working conditions have led to the removal of many potential dangers to health. The result has been a significant reduction in accidents and a lower number of work-related illnesses. Nowadays, most health problems are related to physical support and bodily movement areas or are of a psychosomatic nature. This makes new demands on health and safety work, which now concentrates less on classical health protection and more on promotion of health and personality development.

This new approach is articulated at Volkswagen by the promotion of healthy workplaces and the active involvement of the workforce in health and safety matters. By sharing responsibility in this field they are able to contribute towards modern health promotion within the company.

Nowadays, organisation of work starts at the product development stage, and with the planning of new plants and machinery. A series of measures are involved, all of which are aimed at encouraging appropriate patterns of behaviour. Various innovations, such as ergonomic design of the workplace, health circles, safety audits and health coaching, have contributed towards bringing health and safety standards at Volkswagen up to a very high level.

Volkswagen's aim is to maximise the competitive edge to be gained from having high standards of health. To achieve this it has defined global objectives for the state of health of its workforce throughout the world. In terms of attendance records – admittedly not an absolute measure of state of health – the aim is to achieve a quota of 96%-97%.

Within Germany, Volkswagen leads its competitors in the automotive industry with 96%. A benchmarking project involving Volkswagen and almost 30 other companies has revealed that in all cases, a significant contribution towards reducing absenteeism can be made by talking directly to the workforce. Those returning to work can be engaged in discussions – on a one-to-one basis or in groups – on possible causes of high absenteeism, and steps can be taken to tackle these.

The common objective: promoting a consistently high "health quota".

Of course, presence at work is not always synonymous with good health – a diabetic who comes to work every day is an example of this – and absence from work is not always synonymous with genuine illness. Only if individuals, the management, the works council and the medical service work together can a high "health quota" be achieved in the long term. It goes without saying that anyone who is genuinely ill should receive appropriate care. Those who are in good health turn up for work and don't let their fellow team members down – thus contributing to the company's competitiveness.

An agreement on environmental protection has been signed, with the aim of establishing environmentally compatible working practices. For the first time ever, regulations have been established which involve the workforce directly in environmental protection activities and at the same time establish a mandatory "en-

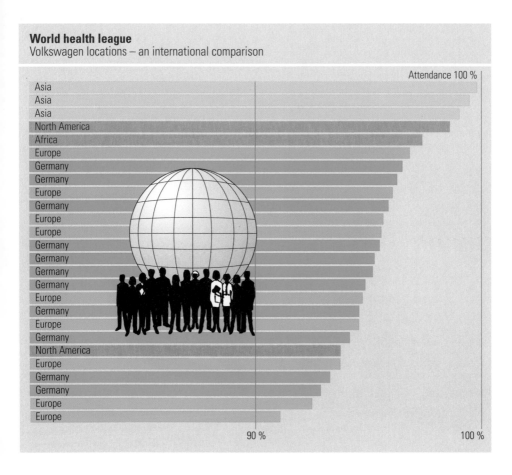

World health league
Volkswagen locations – an international comparison

Attendance 100 %

Asia
Asia
Asia
North America
Africa
Europe
Germany
Germany
Europe
Germany
Europe
Europe
Germany
Germany
Germany
Germany
Europe
Germany
Europe
Germany
North America
Europe
Germany
Germany
Europe
Europe

90 %   100 %

vironmental code of practice" for everyone. The idea is to involve local workforces and works councils in cooperating in the following areas:

- activities to implement the Code of Practice
- preventive measures to avoid environmental damage
- consultation regarding the possible impact on the environment
- vocational training, further training and management training in environmental protection
- election of an environmental officer
- joint environmental audits and environmental protection projects

Protecting the environment has thus become an important element in the typical M4 profile. The agreement underpins the notion of the responsible and committed employee.

Coaching – the route to top performance

No matter how good you are, there is always room for improvement…

The creation of top-quality products requires top-quality performance from all sections of a company. But this does not just happen of its own accord – it needs to be constantly encouraged and promoted. This was the reason for setting up the Volkswagen Coaching Company – as a way of helping to bring the workforce up to the level required by the M4 approach. The notion of coaching underpins the transformation process within the company, the development of appropriate management techniques and the structural reorganisation of work.

The notion of coaching

A truly entrepreneurial approach involves capitalising on the opportunities offered by change. The major challenge facing every company is how to achieve change and increase value-added faster than its rivals. In this context, "faster" means:
- shorter deadlines
- changed priorities
- increased assertiveness
- shorter innovation cycles
- faster communications

Changes in mental attitudes and professional knowledge have to reach the hearts and minds of the workforce more quickly. This is where coaching comes in. Coaching is an attempt to attain a deeper understanding of how individuals or teams achieve top performance. This is the key to identifying and promoting excellence. Experience and observation show that there is nothing as convincing and motivating as a good example set within a team.

The qualities needed to be the sort of team leader required by the Volkswagen approach to management are professionalism, personality and vitality. The idea of coaching is that team leaders are familiarised, step by step, with the basic concept of coaching and then encouraged to lead their own teams to better performance by introducing new ideas, improved procedures and enhanced expertise. Coaching in this form can play a crucial role in successful management of change.

To compete for customers and market share, the VW team has to develop the right attitudes and skills at all levels. "Coaching" is the key.

The idea is to achieve within the company the sort of effect which is well-known, for example, in the world of sport: interaction between broad-based development activities, an enlarged pool of talent and the example set by top performances. Within this basic approach there is an enormous variety of possible ways to apply the principle of coaching to fostering excellence. The concept covers all aspects of performance – specialist knowledge, behaviour and health.

Volkswagen has already made a modest start in this field – with the long-term aim of applying the experience gained to promoting both "talent pools" and employee development in general. Coaching is initially being applied only to individual training measures and team projects, but is intended eventually to form the basis of the company's entire approach to personnel development and training. To this end, all such activities at Volkswagen have been brought together under the umbrella of a newly-founded "Coaching Company".

Volkswagen Coaching Company – concepts for working people

The approach described above was deemed to have such potential that in January 1995 the Volkswagen Coaching Company was set up with an initial budget of DM 120 million. All training and personnel development activities at Volkswagen AG have been restructured along coaching lines, and the activities of the new Coaching Company focus on individual coaching, benchmarking and process planning. Six different organisational units offer their services to Volkswagen – and also external customers.

A branch has been set up at every Volkswagen plant, and cooperation with all Group business locations and local representatives has been agreed on. Starting with vocational and advanced training, a comprehensive strategy with a new focus has been developed. The Volkswagen Coaching Company constitutes a "Centre of Competence" for the Volkswagen Group and is responsible for the introduction of the concept of coaching throughout its global activities. It operates on the basis of a business plan, with a supervisory board consisting of equal numbers of members of the Volkswagen Executive Board and the Central Works Council.

At regional level, the Volkswagen Coaching Company operates as an interface between Volkswagen and the labour market, and is responsible for the selection of trainees and highly-qualified young management replacement candidates, the drawing up of human resource and employment strategies in cases of local restructuring, and the provision of customised coaching for improving skills in particular plants. To achieve this, it works in close cooperation with local labour offices, suppliers and other partners. Thus the local branches of the Volkswagen Coaching Company see their role as that of a kind of regional development agency. They try to open up external markets and improve the quality

Volkswagen Coaching Company Ltd
Business segments

Management development
- Management diagnosis and Personal Development Plan
- Management training and talent pool
- International development and trainee programmes

Primary and advanced training
- Vocational training
- Specialist and general interpersonal training
- Advanced training leading to recognised qualifications

Coaching
- for executives and teams

Corporate consulting for process optimisation
- Organisational development/ process assistance
- Organisation of CIP^2 workshops
- Training of CIP^2 moderators

Labour market and social policy projects
- Subsidised training and retraining Support of insourcing/ outsourcing projects
- Consultation for labour market initiatives
- Support for new businesses and business parks

Benchmarking
- Identification of developments and trends in personnel work and management (world standard) in Europe, the USA and Asia

of services by their very closeness to the market. The approach proved successful within the very first year of the company's existence, and the Coaching Company soon made a name for itself with a series of measures such as vocational training for other companies, retraining measures in conjunction with labour offices, process consultancy and management development, and one-off services provided to authorities and institutions.

Under the heading "Volkswagen Coaching – Focusing on Professional Needs" an important contribution to enhancing competitiveness is expected:
- the development and promotion of excellence
- support for transformation processes
- the further development and promotion of the new M4 Employee concept
- the minimisation of the social impact of structural change at the workplace

Coaching for excellence

The most demanding form of coaching on offer consists of individualised training for excellence. This is a highly personalised service, involving initial consultation, selection of a suitable coach, identification of an individual's level of knowledge, establishment of learning objectives, careful planning of timetable and learning tempo, monitoring of progress and debriefing on completion. This form of coaching is offered at management level – i.e. to individuals who have already proved themselves in terms of subject skills, entrepreneurial approach and leadership qualities and who wish to respond to ambitious objectives by improving their existing strengths and developing their personalities.

If you aim high you have to know where you are starting from. To establish this, a self-appraisal is carried out using a questionnaire intended to sensitise the individual to the issues concerned and encourage self-examination. And a 360° audit provides an all-round view of the person from the point of view of customers, colleagues, superiors and staff. This management audit has been tailor-made for VW management and is at present undergoing testing.

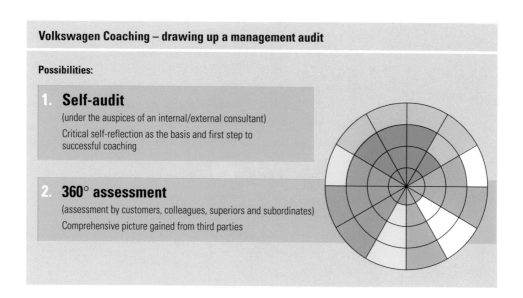

Volkswagen Coaching – drawing up a management audit

Possibilities:

1. Self-audit
(under the auspices of an internal/external consultant)
Critical self-reflection as the basis and first step to successful coaching

2. 360° assessment
(assessment by customers, colleagues, superiors and subordinates)
Comprehensive picture gained from third parties

On the basis of the audit, personal optimisation objectives are then set, and the coaching process begins. The manager involved helps determine the strategy chosen, and can express a preference for a particular coach who he feels will promote the development process most effectively.

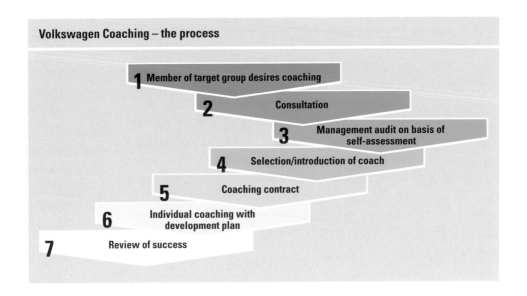

The coaching involves a process of change for the individual concerned, which comes in three stages: the "unfreezing" of old, established patterns of behaviour and perception, the actual process of change, and the "freezing" of new, successful patterns. The example which follows illustrates this.

During initial contacts the coach and manager define their objectives by:

- thoroughly analysing the status quo
- examining the established behavioural patterns of the manager, considering their appropriateness and defining the subject-matter of the coaching topic
- comparing the individual's self-perception with other people's view of him
- establishing priorities for the optimisation process

After this stage of "unfreezing" existing patterns, methods of acquiring new behavioural patterns and knowledge are considered and selected. The choice is a broad one, but not every option is effective. What may be necessary in one case is the acquisition of specialist knowledge or expert personality training, whereas in another what may be more effective is confrontation with live situations in which the coach provides feedback e.g. by "flooding" – constant repetition of the situation concerned.

Afterwards the coach and manager will work together on consolidating new behavioural patterns and then move on to the next step.

Throughout this process, the task of the coach is to provide constructive support – and the demands made on him are extremely high if he is doing his job properly. In addition to possessing subject expertise and displaying a high degree of professionalism, he has to set up a relationship of mutual trust and cooperation with the manager concerned. The choice of coaches reflects the broad spectrum of coaching requirements within the company – they can be subject-specialists or generalists – or outstanding representatives of other companies. But the manager concerned always has the final say in selection of the coach – as the "chemistry" has to be right. Successful businessmen are always of particular interest as top coaches. Cooperation is easier to achieve if Board members and top managers from Volkswagen are responsible for coaching managers from their own company. One-to-one coaching – from which both parties benefit – opens up new scope for increasing efficiency. This is only the start of an exciting new road to excellence which builds on existing high levels of performance.

The Volkswagen Coaching Company ensures the professionalism and subject-related competencies of its coaches through careful selection and multiple assessment. Close coordination and consultation between the VW coaches aids the further development of the coaching concept.

Initial results of a survey of VW managers who have undergone coaching confirm that the company was right to develop this idea. The majority of those consulted considered the success rate in achieving goals was unusually high. More than half spoke of

100% success – thereby confirming that "there is always room for improvement...". There was general agreement that coaching represents an effective service offered by Volkswagen.

Another measure consists of regular surveys of top managers and experts to establish how requirements have changed and where new emphasis has to be made. All this information flows into the personal development plans for management:

Six to ten sessions with the coach, usually over a period of six months, form the first phase of development, aimed at:

- *encouraging innovation*
- *increasing one's own flexibility*
- *making better use of the workforce's potential*
- *breaking down resistance to new ideas*
- *increasing one's own efficiency*

- personality coaching and individual advice based on the 360° audit;
- professional coaching, particularly prior to taking on new tasks: for example a future foundry manager of a company in the Group undergoes individualised coaching within the Group, its suppliers, future customers and the competition, and is brought up to date with regard to the latest processes, machinery, mechanical processing, process control and quality assurance;
- health coaching to guarantee fitness and ability to cope with stress.

In addition to participating in this comprehensive programme, the individual manager also takes part in International Management Development Programmes consisting of seminars and project-work. In the company's "International Management Training and Communications Centre", at Haus Rhode, more than 40 different management seminars per year are organised on a variety of topics, ranging from the new – "Thinking in Networks", "Change Management", "Neurolinguistic Programming" and "Outdoor Training" – to the more traditional "Total Quality Management".

Then there are group coaching programmes aimed not just at encouraging excellence but also at promoting international cohesion within the Volkswagen World: the Group Junior Executive Programme, the Group Executive Forum and the Group Top Management Conference. These events, which complement the one-on-one coaching described above, also culminate in the drawing up of personal action plans (albeit as the result of group discussions), which aim to use the commitment of the workforce to achieve significant changes in the Volkswagen Group.

Health coaching

Apart from coaching aimed at changing attitudes and improving specialist skills – on a one-to-one basis and in groups – Volkswagen has also developed the concept of health coaching. Health and fitness are a necessary basis for sustained, high-level performance. The underlying idea of health coaching is that of long-term supervision and monitoring involving regular check-ups in the Company Health Centre and the drawing up of individualised health profiles and health plans for managers and other groups subject to high levels of stress. Appropriate medical measures can then be taken – or individual psychological and physical training (relaxation and exercise programmes).

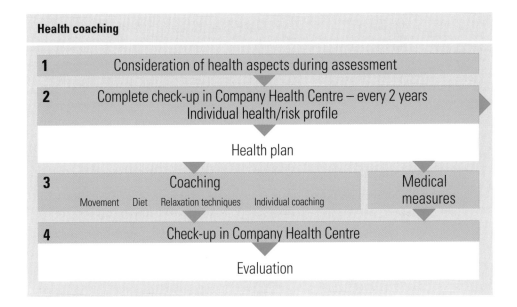

Health coaching

| 1 | Consideration of health aspects during assessment |
| 2 | Complete check-up in Company Health Centre – every 2 years
Individual health/risk profile |

Health plan

| 3 | Coaching
Movement   Diet   Relaxation techniques   Individual coaching | Medical measures |
| 4 | Check-up in Company Health Centre |

Evaluation

Primary and advanced training

Coaching for managers and specialists is only one element in a comprehensive training strategy for M4 Employees within the company. High-flying training programmes can provide insights and methods which are also useful for broad-based development.

Various elements, ranging from the selection procedure to the personal development plan, have already been used well beyond management circles. Basically, what is good for management is good for everyone.

Primary and advanced training play a particularly important role within the Coaching Company.

Using modern technology centres, self-study facilities, laboratories and tried-and-tested teaching techniques, Volkswagen provides a modern, needs-oriented, primary training for new recruits and also subject-specific and general advanced training for existing staff. Practically-oriented teaching methods are combined with personality development measures.

Volkswagen is actively discussing the future of the dual system of vocational training, with a view to putting greater emphasis in future on key elements such as teamwork and establishing closer links between the vocational training institute and the plant.

Apprenticeships are provided in 18 different trades and skills, ranging from "classic" metalworking and electrical subjects, such as industrial mechanics or electronics, to business courses for executive and office workers.

Several hundred different seminars and courses are offered as part of the advanced training programme. These are divided into – Technical courses: hydraulics, pneumatics, microprocessors, CNC technology; Communication and Management courses: rhetoric, presentation methods, management techniques; EDP courses: Windows applications, CAD and Law, Economics and Languages courses: English, Spanish, labour law, business economics. In the long term, fewer standard courses and more specific, tailor-made solutions will be called for. And for the M4 Employee as well, the relationship between time spent on working and time spent on training will change, as the workforce gains greater control over its working hours. Already there is an increasing trend towards training courses being taken outside working hours. The further development of each employee will be documented in his Personal Development Plan. Multiple qualifications and mobility-enhancing attributes such as language skills will then be stored on a "talent database" and enable suitable candidates for group projects and foreign assignments to be rapidly identified.

Corporate consulting for process optimisation

Another area of activity of the Volkswagen Coaching Company is the provision of consultancy services to customers wishing to optimise their business processes.

The changes occurring in organisations – like CIP^2, work groups, restructuring of business processes, simultaneous engineering etc. – require a familiarity with systems and process-plan-

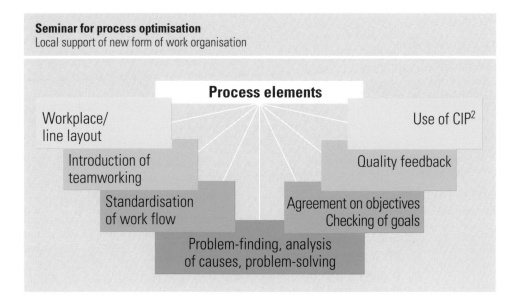

Seminar for process optimisation
Local support of new form of work organisation

Process elements

Workplace/ line layout

Use of CIP^2

Introduction of teamworking

Quality feedback

Standardisation of work flow

Agreement on objectives Checking of goals

Problem-finding, analysis of causes, problem-solving

ning procedures. Experienced advice is essential if the process of change within a company is to be successful. This can take the form of support, consultancy, training, mediation, organisation and coordination. Such measures are aimed at employees and management at all levels, work teams and organisational units – as well as systems and processes. The aim is to provide support in analysing and solving the customer's specific problems. One of the main functions in this context is the provision of advice for projects and measures aimed at changing organisational structures and processes. One instrument used is the so-called "Coaching-Car Seminar", which uses simulation techniques to support the preparation and introduction of new forms of work organisation based on teamwork and shop-floor management. As in the CIP^2

workshops, the transfer from one layout to another is worked out with the participation of everyone involved, drawing on practical experience in production, administration (e.g. Volkswagen Bank), research and development and marketing. As global vehicle strategies develop, there is a growing need for the provision of training to back up the introduction, development and manufacture of new products. Here there is valuable experience available from the many new plants set up during the period of expansion of the Group. Advisors can play a key role in transformation processes and the introduction of new, optimised procedures – and their selection and training is set to become increasingly important.

Personnel research and benchmarking

A forward-looking personnel policy aimed at achieving a "new approach" needs to be based not only on practical experience but also on a properly researched scientific foundation. Efficiency demands that innovative approaches to personnel policy are identified quickly throughout the world, investigated, measured against present practice and then rapidly implemented within the Volkswagen Group. Systematic in-house personnel research helps provide an overview of the latest developments in the field. Personnel managers at Volkswagen form a team which has to compete, like all others – and this means accepting that many personnel managers throughout the world do certain things better than they do. But it also means being determined to find out why this is the case and to learn from it! Benchmarking has an important role to play when new ideas are being developed for the future. Benchmarking makes it easier to see how things are done elsewhere and then to implement everything yourself. It replaces the management consultant, and represents a comprehensive and systematic approach to improving the processes within your company. An essential element here is the ability to learn from and with others. It is more than just a question of comparing figures – benchmarking is a universal process. Our own benchmarking process consists of seven stages:

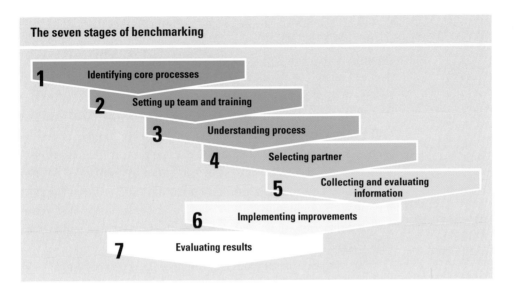

The seven stages of benchmarking

1 Identifying core processes

2 Setting up team and training

3 Understanding process

4 Selecting partner

5 Collecting and evaluating information

6 Implementing improvements

7 Evaluating results

First the core processes are identified and their perform-ance, value-added elements and value to the customer are as-sessed. This is then used as a basis for establishing the objectives of the benchmarking project, and forming the appropriate team, which is then given a thorough introduction to the philosophy and methods of benchmarking. Processes are documented and made measurable – which helps reveal structures and links. With a vir-tual team and contacts with companies at home and abroad, those companies are identified which are "best in process". A precise checklist and guidelines ensure that the correct informa-tion is recorded and methods for improvement are developed. The end result is a precisely-determined list of measures, imple-mentation of which is supported and the degree of success care-fully monitored.

The first projects to have been launched are:
- improvement of health levels
- optimisation of international assignments
- optimisation of management planning
- improvement of communications between marketing and the dealer organisation
- process optimisation of machinery and toolmaking

The results of these projects confirm that benchmarking really offers an effective way of ensuring that the best ideas are identified and adopted as rapidly as possible.

Labour market and social policy projects

This area of activity forms part of the interface between Volkswagen and the labour market. Innovative models of the labour market are developed, and the scope for introducing promotional measures is investigated individually. Services on offer range from subsidised training and retraining measures, support for insourcing/outsourcing projects, and consultancy over manpower policy initiatives, right down to the provision of support for new companies and industrial estates.

To support further development of the regional infrastructure and create a bridge between Volkswagen and the labour market, the Volkswagen Coaching Company offers graduates of universities and specialist colleges the opportunity to gain 18 months' experience through practical placements in the various specialist divisions of the company. During this period they are involved in specific projects such as, for example, the development of a new production plant or the marketing of a new product. At

Labour market and social policy projects

Measures to safeguard employment	Measures to retain competitiveness	Further development of regional infrastructure
• Manpower Assignment Centres • Promotion of training and retraining • Support for insourcing/outsourcing projects	• Support for regional employment adjustment • Inter-plant training • Early-warning system for identification of structural problems	• Employment policy plans for region (cooperation with RESON – Regional Development Agency for Lower Saxony) • Support for measures to preserve existing businesses and found new ones

the same time they attend seminars and receive individual coaching. This is a way of overcoming a freeze on new recruitment. Those taking part gain invaluable experience, pick up new ideas and increase their chances of finding a conventional job.

The Volkswagen Coaching Company has developed into a service-provider vis-à-vis local labour market authorities. A number of retraining and advanced training measures have either already been launched or are in preparation. These programmes, which are run by the six branches of the Coaching Company, last for up to two years and are designed for individuals as well as whole groups.

Structural change in European industry means that different types of training and qualifications are now in demand. Here, cooperation with European partners makes sense. Involvement in projects within the ADAPT and LEONARDO programmes enables the European dimension of labour market change to be taken into account. What are the implications throughout Europe of the changes occurring in the automotive industry for flexibility, mobility and quality of work?

The philosophy of the Coaching Company can be summed up as: "concepts for working people" – which reflects the breadth of services it offers to companies, administrations and organisations, even outside the automotive industry. With a staff of almost 500, every customer can be offered a tailor-made, innovative solution which helps increase the flexibility of the company concerned and allows the full potential of its workforce and management to be realised.

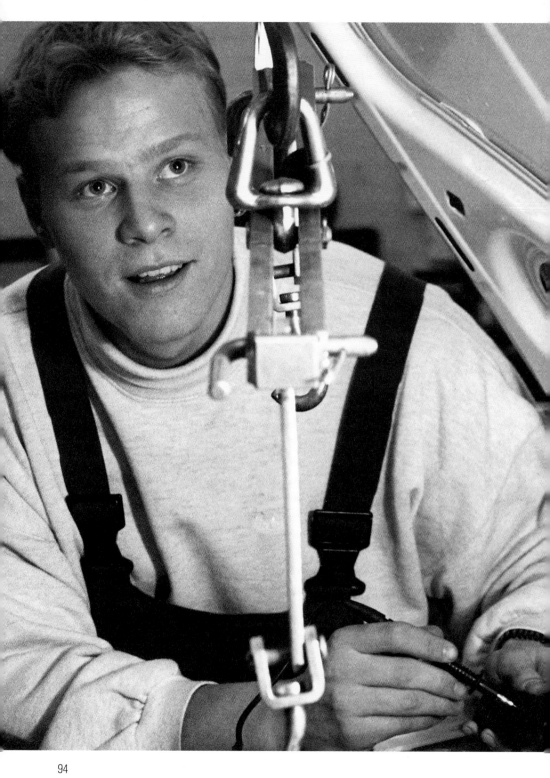

The variability of the employment relationship

Redefining the value of jobs

Most people's ultimate goal is still to have a full-time job. But when work is in short supply a better alternative to unemployment is a redistribution, redefinition and sharing of existing jobs. It is therefore important for society to place a higher value on variable working times and new forms of employment relationships than has been the case up till now. In terms both of remuneration and psychology, the relationship between a company and its workforce offers much more scope for creative approaches than has been assumed in the past. It is possible to considerably increase the variety of types of employment contract offered.

The new variability

Throughout the world, mass unemployment has become one of the most pressing problems of modern times. The automotive industry has been hit by a crisis of restructuring and excess capacity. It would have been easy enough for Volkswagen to follow the example of many other companies and simply shed jobs. But as "Every Job has a Face", the company therefore decided, in the autumn of 1993, to break out of the vicious circle of mass unemployment. It is all very well for market trends, technological progress or productivity to define personnel requirements – but these factors alone should not be allowed to dictate the nature of the solution to the problem.

The question which Volkswagen faced in 1993 was: how to rapidly reduce a cost factor running to billions of Deutschmarks which was already being undermined by the intense pressure of competition.

The question facing Volkswagen was a personnel policy issue: how does one convert some 100,000 jobs into 70,000 jobs, which are all that are required to cover existing oranisational needs?

The only way to achieve this was to play the diversity card. Every possible contribution towards solving such an intractable problem was taken seriously. Developing the Volkswagen Model required everyone to be allowed to give free rein to their imagination and resourcefulness. One thing was clear though – without some degree of shortening and redistribution of working time it would not be possible to solve the problem. The variants developed could cover days, weeks, months or years – even entire working lives.

Certain fundamental questions had to be answered in this context:

- What should a job with a built-in variable time element look like in terms of material benefits and social value, if it is to convince employees who have spent their entire working lives in "normal" posts that it enjoys a similar – or at least an "acceptable" – degree of recognition?
- What are the factors which influence people when they choose between variable and "normal" employment?

- What significance does variable employment have for future labour markets, and what form could it take?

It is usually difficult to change people's basic attitudes. But if variable forms of employment are to be accepted as such, then the value attached to work and jobs must change and be charged with the associations hitherto reserved for full-time employment. Before introducing such a dramatic change into the world of work at Volkswagen, questions like these had to be discussed, so that the people involved could develop a new attitude towards work and forms of employment.

What value do people in Germany attach to their jobs, and what conditions are they prepared to accept in order to secure them?

The new value of jobs

The value of a job is measured primarily in material terms – in other words the fact that it provides an income which is acceptable to the employee concerned and affordable for the employer. But a job also has a psychological value. It boosts an individual's confidence and helps integrate him into society. Both these aspects – the material and the psychological – are important, but the latter looms larger in the case of variable forms of employment, the "variable" employee is no longer blindly following the usual route – he has made a conscious decision, either personally or in conjunction with workforce representatives, to relinquish part of his work. In future every employee, before launching into variable employment, will ask himself: what is an acceptable contribution from my point of view, and to what extent, in a competitive situation, can I safeguard my job in the long term? There is a growing preparedness to look at jobs in a new light, for many people are increasingly realising just how important work is in social terms. In a high-wage economy a job in industry has a social and cultural value, and if they wish to preserve it then they must be prepared to make certain sacrifices. This new value of jobs has to stand up to market competition and hold its own when viewed by other work cultures.

The value people attach to jobs in automotive plants and their understanding of what employment means is expressed in many different ways all over the world. Some work cultures – especially the Japanese – stress uniformity – from the common de-

97

sign of overalls to the uniform workplace in an open-plan office. Privileges and wage differentials are highly restricted. Other – more European – work cultures have put more emphasis on individual differentiation in the past – whether in terms of clothing, status or wages. The expectation attached to the "uniformity" model – which the Japanese have deliberately applied in their European and American plants – is that uniform types of employment will lead to greater commitment on the part of the employees. They are linked, for example, with a promise of lifetime employment.

It is this obviously highly successful model against which variable employment has to survive in international competition. The prospects of success would seem to be good – given that in Europe it is being applied to work cultures which have always based their success on more individualistic lifestyles, needs and patterns of behaviour. The Japanese work culture would have much greater difficulty in implementing such a drastic adjustment of manpower requirements through variation of the forms of employment on offer.

In introducing variable forms of employment, Volkswagen was able to build on certain stable values: a level of wages virtually unrivalled in the region, a high level of social benefits, and finally a strong sense of security – as the jobs concerned had hitherto always carried life-long guarantees. The level of loyalty to the company was – and is – unusually high.

All these values have made Volkswagen such an attractive employer that applicants have often tended to put greater stress on working for the company than on the type of job concerned. This is an attitude which can be found running through all personnel work at Volkswagen. However exciting the offer of an outside job may be, and whatever its importance in career terms, employees find it very difficult to hand in their notice at Volkswagen – even if they are merely transferring within the Group.

The battles over the framework agreement with the works council on the introduction of an early retirement plan were fought against this background. VW employees wanted to retain the feeling that they were leaving the company by a generally accepted route without actually ever quitting the extended community which it represented. This feeling often compensated for the mixed feelings with which individuals relinquished their jobs in return for severance pay of sixty or a hundred thousand Deutschmarks.

The new relationship with the company

This high level of commitment and social standards offered a chance to deliberately extend the range and number of variable forms of employment offered in 1993, in a bid to prevent the enforced layoffs of some 30,000 employees. The secure financial circumstances of many of those involved meant that they were in a position to accept the offer of variable employment. The idea was to use the scope offered by this situation to redefine their relationship with the company. It was possible to attach a much higher value to having a job, security and good prospects for the future in a company like Volkswagen.

Many employees nowadays have much greater room to manoeuvre than the previous generation did – and this is not just thanks to Volkswagen. More than fifty years of peace have allowed many families to amass property and wealth, while at the same time financial burdens have in many cases been reduced – for example by the trend towards smaller families.

Thus the introduction of variable forms of employment went well beyond the mere sharing out of work during a crisis. It was all about the psychological links – security, care, protection, support and involvement which can be offered to individuals. In other words – the long term bonds which link people with each other, with other generations with their neighbours and with Volkswagen, and which give them the confidence to make full use of the variables on offer – from full-time working to full-time release from work with an option of re-employment by the company. These psychological links can embrace the entire workforce, whether they are working full-time or on a block-release or phased working basis. It is the feeling of being able to leave and return which makes an extended relationship and greater variability acceptable.

Even employees who go to work for suppliers as part of a strategic insourcing project retain their psychological links with Volkswagen. In material terms, employment at Volkswagen may cease with termination of their contract, but the joint effort of manufacturing a Volkswagen product makes all suppliers part of the extended Volkswagen Family. After all, 90% of car manufacture – the lion's share – consists of upstream production prior to actual assembly.

An important element in this redefinition of work within variable forms of employment is the development process within the job itself. New activities and instruments like CIP[2], teamwork or cost centres offer everyone greater scope to become involved – a greater sense of "ownership", a feeling that their work is worthwhile.

What is called for is long-term cohesion and solidarity within the company. How much is the workforce prepared to contribute towards preserving the high quality of life which a job at Volkswagen offers mothers, fathers and children?

The individual can incorporate this higher significance of work into his own personal calculations. Success at work is thus redefined. In the future, greater importance will be attached to work as a contribution to the success of the entire community – in other words there will be an increase in the value-added element of work – and the protection of one's job in a national industry will become more important.

Responsibility and variability are set to loom larger in personnel work, too. They offer an opportunity to become more actively involved in a variety of employment situations, and to regain the feeling of being able to influence one's own fate.

New forms of relationships with companies

Variability of employment can take several forms. For example a full-time contract with Volkswagen, or an employment relationship in a broader sense, in which one's personal career plans are based on Volkswagen.

There are many different possibilities within the lifespan of an individual Volkswagen employee. He can be integrated into employment directly after training via the phased working programme, which allows him to build up his working hours until he reaches the normal quota for the plant concerned.

Several block periods during professional life could in principle offer opportunities to undergo further training to enhance performance, or to retrain for a different kind of work. Demand-

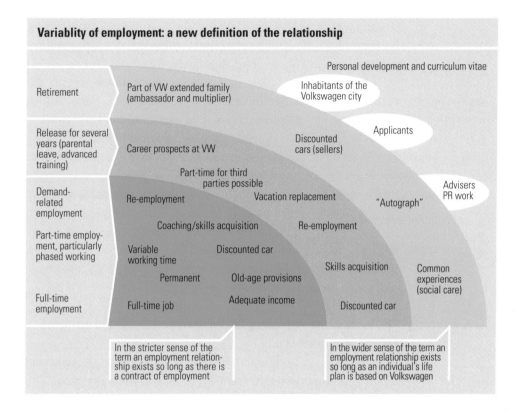

Variablity of employment: a new definition of the relationship

Personal development and curriculum vitae

Retirement

Part of VW extended family (ambassador and multiplier)

Inhabitants of the Volkswagen city

Release for several years (parental leave, advanced training)

Career prospects at VW

Discounted cars (sellers)

Applicants

Part-time for third parties possible

Advisers PR work

Demand-related employment

Re-employment

Vacation replacement

"Autograph"

Coaching/skills acquisition

Re-employment

Part-time employment, particularly phased working

Variable working time

Discounted car

Skills acquisition

Common experiences (social care)

Permanent

Old-age provisions

Full-time employment

Full-time job

Adequate income

Discounted car

In the stricter sense of the term an employment relationship exists so long as there is a contract of employment

In the wider sense of the term an employment relationship exists so long as an individual's life plan is based on Volkswagen

related employment on an annual basis would offer greater scope, for example, to pursue further educational studies in parallel or to take on some form of voluntary work. Job sharing by couples starting a family – a "phased working programme for parents" – could be more easily realised than in the past. "If I have a feeling of belonging, then I don't mind staying away for some time!" A job at Volkswagen can provide stability and encourage more people to make more active use of opportunities and interests which crop up in their lives – always with the knowledge that they are giving more people the possibility of employment.

This allows a constant movement between the inner circle of those working at Volkswagen at any one time and the larger, outer circle of the Volkswagen workforce, which is largely made up of employees who have been released from work, transferred to work for suppliers, or have retired but remain within the extended Volkswagen community. Thus, despite its reduced internal labour market, Volkswagen still has the possibility of maintaining large numbers of employment relationships and can, as needs be, fall back on this source of appropriately skilled employees.

This new relationship extends also to the wider environment of the plants – the family, neighbourhood, and friends of the employees.

Throughout the extended Volkswagen Family small-scale employment pacts can be made – a phased hand-over of work between generations, families and neighbours.

Variability of employment thus also guarantees a turnover of personnel for the future, preventing the workforce from becoming rigid and inflexible. The more this variability allows new, positive forms of living to emerge – "more time for myself – for the children – for social activities – for culture", the stronger this new form of link with Volkswagen becomes. The route embarked on in 1993 constitutes a massive social experiment.

The binding and separating forces operating within the variable employment relationship

As soon as permanent employment problems emerge, the amount of voluntary fluctuation reduces to virtually zero. The more insecure jobs become, the more people cling to them. It is only then that one becomes aware of the benefits which individuals derive from their jobs throughout their entire working lives. Even if they face the most inhumane working conditions, people will defend their jobs tooth and nail as soon as they come under any threat. The unemployed lead less active and varied lives than those in jobs. Often they simply let themselves go. This disturbing conclusion was reached as far back as the world economic crisis in the twenties, by a classic study carried out in the town of Marienthal, which had 100% unemployment.

Work makes people feel useful – and this feeling has to be maintained under variable forms of employment right through to the extended circle of all those associated with Volkswagen, by special personal support and involvement, for example via the company magazine, special discounts on cars, or the organisation of joint events.

Job-rotation, for example in order to prepare people as deputies, or to give them responsibilities within a specific project,

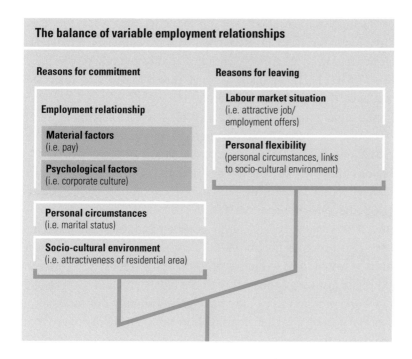

The balance of variable employment relationships

Reasons for commitment

Reasons for leaving

Employment relationship

Labour market situation
(i.e. attractive job/
employment offers)

Material factors
(i.e. pay)

Psychological factors
(i.e. corporate culture)

Personal flexibility
(personal circumstances, links
to socio-cultural environment)

Personal circumstances
(i.e. marital status)

Socio-cultural environment
(i.e. attractiveness of residential area)

can boost the energies operating within the company – even for part-time employees.

This traditionally high degree of loyalty to the Volkswagen Family forms an important asset which can ensure that members of the workforce with important skills are not lost in times of crisis. But despite this, willingness to leave the company will grow, depending on an individual's market value.

As a result of court judgements, a clear view of the factors governing an individual's relationship with his employer has evolved, and been brought to bear especially on cases related to protection against dismissal and selection of candidates for lay-offs. When such dismissal programmes have been drawn up in the past, emphasis has always been put on individuals who have poor chances of finding re-employment, extensive obligations to-wards family or relatives, or are of advanced age. And when cas-es came to court, these criteria were always given priority over factors like company loyalty based on long service.

In other words, when legal decisions are being made it tends to be social criteria which protect an employee from termination or fluctuation of employment. But this does not necessarily have anything to do with a positive bond with the company. Experience shows that even those who were dissatisfied with their jobs have, in the past, been reluctant to leave them. In the long term this would lead to a situation whereby the company was left with a highly unfavourable workforce structure. It is an argument which – in addition to the financial aspects – speaks most against mass reductions and in favour of variable forms of employment. If a major company like Volkswagen initiated a workforce reduction plan aimed at minimising hardship, it would end up losing precisely the generation of workers on whom it has to build its future. There are at present some 30,000 employees under the age of thirty – precisely the number of people who the 1993 figures indicated would need to be laid off. And this is not even considering the explosive social effects this would have in a multicultural society. Foreign workers usually have greater family obligations and therefore enjoy a higher degree of protection from dismissal than many German workers (40% of whom are unmarried!). Variable forms of employment offer scope for adapting the work relationship to the personal situation of the individual without causing such potential divisions in the workforce.

The danger of an increasing willingness to leave the company grows mainly amongst those who are in any case much in demand on the labour market. Here the Coaching Company has a special role to play in cultivating the pool of talent, retaining valuable employees and ensuring that they receive promotion at the appropriate moment.

Nevertheless the mobile employee who fits the M4 profile is still liable to be head-hunted. Managers whose annual salary has been reduced will also tend to respond favourably to attractive job offers made to them.

This is why it is all the more important for the company to offer its employees long-term prospects which go beyond the here-and-now.

The feeling which the Volkswagen personnel philosophy puts across should be one of "belonging to the family".

Changing patterns of commitment

Past	Future
Material	● Adequate income
	● Competition-related remuneration
● Good pay	● Discounted car
● Salary increments	● Pension provisions
● Social benefits	● Social benefits
● Discounted cars	
● Pension provisions	● Dynamic, innovative company
	● Supervision/coaching
	● Self-esteem
Psychological	● Re-employment
● Job security	● Personal development
● Volkswagen Family	● Scope for involvement and
● Tradition	joint decision-making
● Identification/pride	● Volkswagen Family
● Myth	● Identification/pride
● Trust	● Trust

The basic 1993 models: 4-day week, block time and phased working programmes

It took some 40 years to establish the 40-hour week, whereas the 4-day week was agreed within a matter of weeks towards the end of 1993 and implemented at the beginning of 1994. Above all, it was the cost situation which dictated this pace of change.

A workforce reduction plan involving 30,000 employees would have cost Volkswagen many millions of Deutschmarks. And short time working would also have involved heavy costs estimated at DM 500 million.

But the state, too – especially the social security system, and ultimately therefore those paying contributions – would also have had to carry a heavy burden of costs. Short time working payments for 30,000 employees would alone have cost some DM 3.3 million per day. Over the whole of the 1994 working year that would have meant a total cost of some DM 660 million. Unemployment benefit for 30,000 people for several years would have added up to billions. Thus, over the two-year period covered by the collective agreement the national economy would have had to shoulder an additional net burden of over DM 4 billion.

The decision Volkswagen reached was to opt for reductions in the working week without compensation for loss of earnings, based on new models of working time.

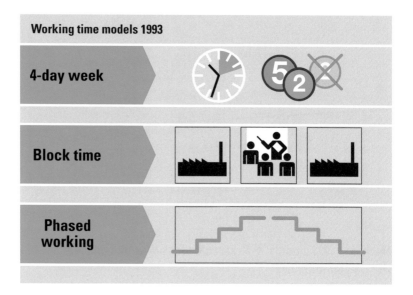

Working time models 1993

4-day week

Block time

Phased working

This introduction of the 4-day week for all 100,000 employees reduced labour costs approximately by 15%. It was a convincing result.

It soon became clear that this had been the best option available. It was appropriate for the particular situation the company found itself in, and was compatible with the basic concept of acceptability for the workforce and the surrounding region.

Model 1: the 4-day week for all

In November 1993 Volkswagen AG launched negotiations with the metalworkers union IG Metall – the largest union within the company – with the aim of achieving agreement on a reduction in working time for the entire workforce without compensation for loss of earnings.

It very quickly became clear that both parties involved in the negotiations regarded securing employment for 100,000 employees as a top priority. But the problem was how to find a compromise which would be acceptable to both sides. On the one hand it was important to keep the financial burden on the workforce to an acceptable size, but on the other hand the company had to achieve the necessary reduction in labour costs to remain competitive and to cope with the slump in demand caused by recession.

In essence, Volkswagen's proposal involved reducing the average working week by 20% from 36 to 28.8 hours, with a simultaneous reduction in earnings for the entire workforce.

The theoretical reduction in monthly income resulting from this move was, however, compensated for by a redistribution of other income elements, the result being that monthly income remained at the levels agreed at the end of October 1993. It was an acceptable solution.

How was it achieved?

In order to understand how such a settlement was possible, it is necessary to examine the various elements which made up the annual income of an employee at Volkswagen at the time. The most important of these were:

- monthly salary
- a special one-off annual payment amounting to 96% of a twelfth of the gross annual salary earned during the previous year
- holiday pay over and above the monthly salary – which continued to be paid during holidays; in simplified terms, this amounted to some 70% of the average gross monthly salary, and was paid on two fixed dates
- a Christmas bonus calculated according to the number of years' service in the company

Two of the three one-off payments – the additional holiday pay and the special annual payment – were of such a size in relation to the monthly salary that they were suitable for redistribution on a monthly basis.

The special payment was completely distributed on a monthly basis, while a residual element of the additional holiday allowance – a uniform sum for all employees – was retained as a one-off payment.

This redistribution was, however, not enough to achieve the desired effect, and two pay rises taking effect on 1 January 1994 were therefore also included in the calculation. The first was a 3.5% increase which had been agreed on 1 November 1993 but subsequently suspended for two months; and the second was an advance payment of 1% in anticipation of the collective bargaining result of 1 August 1994.

In addition to this, the agreed introduction of the 35-hour week on 1 October 1995 with full compensation for loss of earnings was brought forward. And the next element in the package was the abolition of the so-called "recuperative holiday". This was a measure introduced in the fifties by the then Chairman of the Board, Heinrich Nordhoff, with the intention of providing some compensation for the extreme physical strain suffered by people during the post-war period of national reconstruction.

The sum of all these elements was, however, still not enough to compensate completely for the reduction in monthly income, so the company, as part of the compromise it was proposing, added a sum equal to approximately 2% of monthly income in order finally to achieve a balance.

A specific example

It was a complex calculation, which the media often referred to as the "secret formula" of the Volkswagen solution. It is perhaps most easily explained using as an example a monthly income on the "F"-level of the wage scale. This is the category into which most of the employees in the direct production sector fall, and also some in indirect areas such as administration, transport and logistics.

New monthly wage according to the 4-day week model

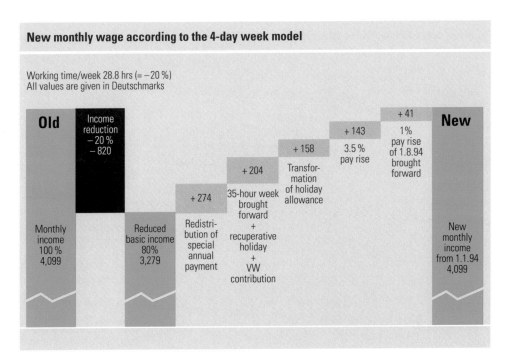

Working time/week 28.8 hrs (= −20 %)
All values are given in Deutschmarks

Old — Monthly income 100 % 4,099

Income reduction −20 % −820

Reduced basic income 80% 3,279

+274 Redistribution of special annual payment

+204 35-hour week brought forward + recuperative holiday + VW contribution

+158 Transformation of holiday allowance

+143 3.5 % pay rise

+41 1% pay rise of 1.8.94 brought forward

New — New monthly income from 1.1.94 4,099

At the time the monthly income, for example of an assembly worker, was DM 4,099. A reduction of 20% would have brought this down to DM 3,279. However, thanks to the redistribution and transfer of various elements of annual income – including the special annual payment of DM 274 as the biggest element – this was brought back up to its original level.

Thus each individual employee was able to continue to meet his monthly expenditure – which was an important element in persuading the workforce to accept the 4-day week.

Of course the workforce had to make certain sacrifices as far as overall annual income was concerned. The actual reduction in income over the year for each individual depended on the salary scale and tax-band involved. Overall, however, one can say that the average reduction in net annual income was 12%. Added to this is the pay-rise from the 1993 round of collective bargaining, which had been included in the calculation and therefore did not apply. The "recuperative holiday" also disappeared permanently as a cost factor.

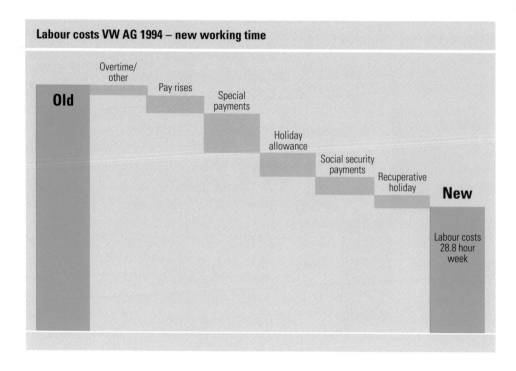

Labour costs VW AG 1994 – new working time

Old

Overtime/other

Pay rises

Special payments

Holiday allowance

Social security payments

Recuperative holiday

New

Labour costs 28.8 hour week

The company had set itself the goal of achieving a significant overall reduction of labour costs. Implementation of the model described above led to overall savings of some DM 1.6 billion in 1994. In addition to the elements already described which were included in the calculation of the new monthly income, the lower statutory social security contributions in particular also had a positive effect on the savings.

Model 2: block time programme

A further model was developed in 1993 in the form of a "block time" programme. This was in response to a desire expressed by all sides for more scope to be created for lifelong learning processes. The younger generation, especially, was to be given the chance to upgrade their skills without being put under excessive strain. This model converts the "normal" double load of work and training into a combination which allows the employee scope to work and earn money as well as upgrade his skills over the course of the year. Block time is the key to making this possible.

The demographic development of the VW workforce indicated that this measure offered considerable potential. The target group consisted of all members of the workforce between the ages of 18 and 30, and unmarried employees – making a potential pool of some 42,000 employees in 1994 (and still 37,000 in 1996). The idea was that they would be able to interrupt their working careers, usually for a period of between three and six months.

With the aid of such block time arrangements – in other words a period of unemployment of limited duration used for re-training and skills acquisition – reduction of the workforce, necessary restructuring measures and re-employment in newly-created jobs were linked together in a time plan.

Unfortunately legislation in Germany was amended with the express aim of preventing such models of unemployment of

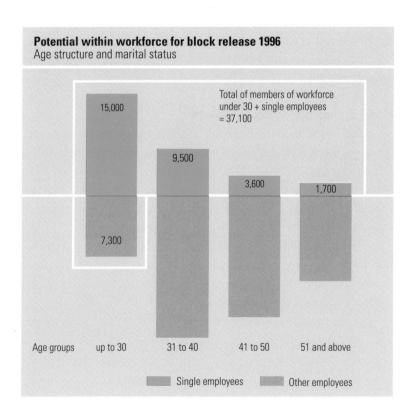

Potential within workforce for block release 1996
Age structure and marital status

Total of members of workforce under 30 + single employees = 37,100

15,000

9,500

3,600

1,700

7,300

Age groups   up to 30   31 to 40   41 to 50   51 and above

Single employees   Other employees

limited-duration with guaranteed re-employment. The legislature feared such an attractive model might be misused and be invoked for every form of structural change taking place in companies. It was a decision which meant that an opportunity was lost to reach long-term agreement with companies in times of crisis to limit periods of unemployment and give the unemployed some hope for the future. At the time, many people had the impression that labour legislation clearly favoured individuals who were unequivocally unemployed rather than measures which were perhaps less clear-cut, but nevertheless designed to offer more effective help.

Despite these legislative obstacles, Volkswagen and IG Metall managed to define the block time model in the hope that such a creative model would inevitably become the focus of interest once again as unemployment continued to grow, and would therefore be reappraised by the legislators at some time in the near future. And this did, indeed, happen early in 1996 in the form of new legislation on phased early retirement. Volkswagen has also introduced a voluntary block release programme with generous promises of re-employment, but without any legal or collectively agreed safeguards.

Model 3: phased working programmes

The third model, involving a progressive increase or decrease of working time, fits in with the idea of Volkswagen being a "family". Older employees are able to gradually withdraw from work and make way for younger ones. This matches the way responsibility within a family is gradually passed on from one generation to the next – an idea which underlies the model.

Precise analysis of the structure of the workforce revealed that there was considerable potential for such a phased approach to working time, in the form of young employees who have just completed their apprenticeships on the one hand, and older employees on the other, who could use this as a method of progressing towards retirement.

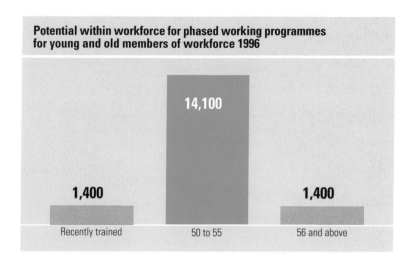

Potential within workforce for phased working programmes for young and old members of workforce 1996

14,100

1,400

1,400

Recently trained 50 to 55 56 and above

The system allows for a working week which progressively increases for freshly qualified employees and – at the other end – is gradually reduced for older employees. It forms a sort of "pact" between the younger and the older generations.

While mother and father, as they grow older, reduce their working week and therefore also their income, the son or daughter can be increasingly integrated into the work process once he or she has completed training.

This phased working programme complements the first two models, and constitutes the most flexible building block within an employment policy aimed at increased responsiveness to demand. These three models basically represented the three most important redistribution instruments available to Volkswagen: reduced, progressively increasing and decreasing working time, and interruptions of limited duration.

The Volkswagen Week

A new approach to working time in
a breathing company

The "Volkswagen Week" – a further development of the 4-day week – is the main contribution which collective agreements have made to the breathing company. In terms of working hours, breathing means making maximum use of flexi-time during the day, greater individual control over working times, and overtime crediting over several years. This is supplemented by the progressive integration of apprentices into full employment and progressive work reduction programmes in the run-up to retirement and through block times and re-entry programmes. The Volkswagen Week utilises a variety of different working time models and forms the central core of our labour relations policy.

The point of departure

At the end of 1993, Volkswagen and the Hanover branch of the metalworkers' union IG Metall, as the parties to the Volkswagen AG company collective agreement, made the headlines. Following negotiations completed in a record 14 days, the negotiating partners had achieved an agreement aimed at safeguarding jobs and company locations which subsequently became known as the "4-day-week".

The agreement reduced standard working hours by 20%, from 36 hours to 28.8 hours per week from January 1994 onwards, in conjunction with a reduction in employees' annual income. A complex calculation system combined with additional allowances meant that monthly pay in fact remained unchanged at October 1993 levels, but special payments of a 13th monthly salary and a large percentage of supplementary holiday pay were dropped. As a result of these changes in pay structure, it was possible to achieve savings in personnel costs of approximately 15%. Thus, existing problems of excess manpower levels had been solved not by the traditional instruments (short time working, reductions in the workforce and mass dismissals) but rather

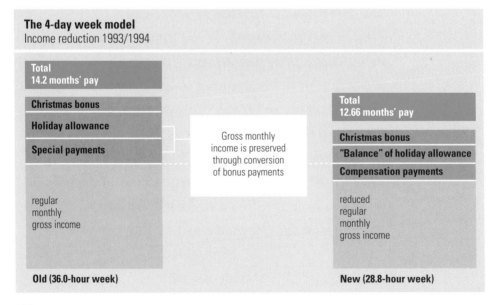

The 4-day week model
Income reduction 1993/1994

Total
14.2 months' pay

Christmas bonus

Holiday allowance

Special payments

regular
monthly
gross income

Gross monthly
income is preserved
through conversion
of bonus payments

Total
12.66 months' pay

Christmas bonus

"Balance" of holiday allowance

Compensation payments

reduced
regular
monthly
gross income

Old (36.0-hour week)   **New (28.8-hour week)**

through a new human resources policy based on the principle of "cutting costs not jobs".

The point of departure of this new approach to human resources policy was a realisation that the continuing recession and the structural problems faced by the automotive industry required a new kind of employment policy. The figures illustrate just how urgently alternative solutions to the issue were required: in 1994 and 1995 approximately 30,000 employees in Volkswagen AG's six plants were surplus to requirements, with 20,000 coming into that category in 1994 alone.

Volkswagen's December 1993 pay agreement took the public by surprise and caused immediate controversy. Reaction at home and abroad among politicians, businessmen, scientists and interested members of the public ranged from outright approval to total rejection. The Volkswagen Model had been developed specifically to resolve the company's own employment problems, but its effects went far beyond Volkswagen. Comparable attempts to find a solution were subsequently made in other sectors, such as the engineering and electrical industries in western Germany and the iron and steel industry and public sector in eastern Germany.

The agreement on the 4-day week safeguarded 20,000 jobs; any additional manpower surpluses were coped with through additional programmes, agreed in May 1994, such as the phased integration of apprentices after training and "work-free block time" (including structural short time working prior to early retirement).

Volkswagen's experience with the 4-day week

The transition from a 36-hour week in 1993 to a 28.8-hour week from 1 January 1994 was time-consuming, difficult and beset with problems. Since the collective agreement only defined the length of the working week but otherwise left a maximum of leeway in specifying how this should be organised, a great deal of negotiation was required at plant level between management and local works councils before the final models of working hours could be implemented. Provisional solutions were agreed in the six plants as an interim arrangement prior to the new models coming into force. These largely involved the shut-down period over Christmas and New Year being lengthened, and plants also closing on certain days during the first quarter of 1994 – as at

Wolfsburg for instance, where the new working time model did not come into force until 4 April 1994.

The end result – given the differing structures, needs and plant capacity requirements – was that the 28.8-hour week was implemented in the form of twelve main models of working hours with approximately 150 smaller scale agreements derived from these. They ranged from straight 4-day models – with a buffer for spare plant capacity on the fifth day – via 5-day models with shorter daily working hours – to multiple shift systems allowing 24-hour plant operation on five days per week. A major advantage for the company was the saving in personnel costs which could be achieved through the 4-day week agreement. But every employee also benefited, as the company agreed not to make any operational layoffs during the period covered by the agreement. In other words, the workforce was given a guarantee of employment – even if only for a set period – which was written into the collective agreement.

A secure job cannot be rated highly enough these days. Public acceptance of the Volkswagen Model was important for future discussions.

A representative survey of a total of 1,001 people throughout Germany carried out by the Gesellschaft für Sozialforschung und statistische Analysen mbH (FORSA) in June 1995 produced the following findings:

The question of whether the Volkswagen Model (shorter working hours and wage reductions) was generally a suitable vehicle for preserving and safeguarding jobs was
- answered positively by 51% of respondents
- answered negatively by 29% of respondents and
- answered with "don't know" by 20% of respondents

An above-average number of state employees (60%) and self-employed people (58%) were of the opinion that the Volkswagen Model was generally applicable. But blue-collar (43%) and white-collar workers (48%) expressed above-average scepticism about the general applicability of the model.

In response to a question about whether they would be personally willing to work less and accept a reduction in wages or salary if that would safeguard jobs,

- more than half (52%) the respondents answered "yes"
- 38% answered "no" and
- a mere 10% answered "don't know"

This positive result is also mirrored in the findings of a representative survey of some 2,600 VW employees in the Wolfsburg, Emden and Brunswick plants carried out in May/June 1995 as part of a project by the Institute for Sociology of the University of Erlangen/Nuremberg. The project was also intended to help prepare for the subsequent collective negotiations.

In response to a question about satisfaction with the 28.8-hour week, almost half the respondents (48.6%) declared themselves "satisfied" or "very satisfied", while a good third (34.7%) answered the question with "partly"; a mere 16.6% were "dissatisfied" or "very dissatisfied". As expected, safeguarding of employment was seen as a key benefit of the 28.8-hour week by a majority of respondents (74%), followed by "more time for the family" (61.4%) and "more leisure time" (60.6%). It is striking that the factor "more leisure time" was highly rated by employees in

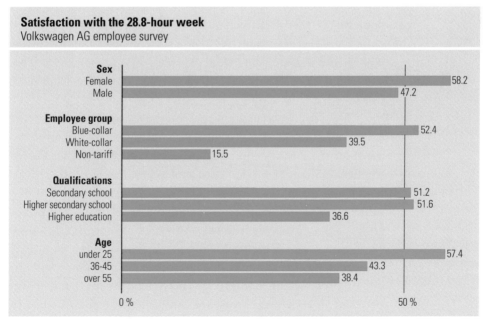

Satisfaction with the 28.8-hour week
Volkswagen AG employee survey

Sex	
Female	58.2
Male	47.2
Employee group	
Blue-collar	52.4
White-collar	39.5
Non-tariff	15.5
Qualifications	
Secondary school	51.2
Higher secondary school	51.6
Higher education	36.6
Age	
under 25	57.4
36-45	43.3
over 55	38.4

Sociology Institute, University of Erlangen/WSI, Düsseldorf

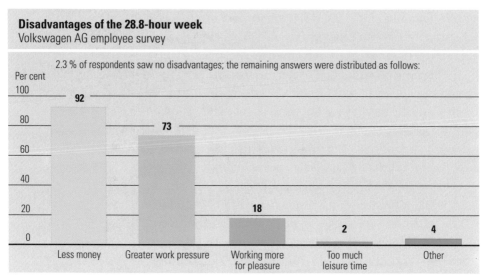

Disadvantages of the 28.8-hour week
Volkswagen AG employee survey

2.3 % of respondents saw no disadvantages; the remaining answers were distributed as follows:

Per cent

92	73	18	2	4
Less money	Greater work pressure	Working more for pleasure	Too much leisure time	Other

Sociology Institute, University of Erlangen/WSI, Düsseldorf

the production sector. A mere 13% of respondents – primarily those in the higher salary groups – were unable to name any benefits resulting from the 28.8-hour week.

In response to a question about "disadvantages of the 28.8-hour week", the most frequent response was – as expected – the associated loss of income (92.3%). A further important disadvantage quoted was increased work pressure (73.4%). Only 2.3% of respondents did not perceive any disadvantages in the 28.8-hour week.

The most surprising information to emerge from this survey came from analysis of the factors influencing the responses to the question about satisfaction with the 28.8-hour week. Since the introduction of the 28.8-hour week was associated with a loss of annual income of about 15%, it might have been expected that dissatisfaction would be greatest among the lower wage and salary groups and households with below-average income. But the opposite was the case. The level of dissatisfaction with the 28.8-hour week increases as the level of a household's net income rises – in other words, with income group. This in turn means that it is precisely employees in the lower and middle income groups who are more willing to accept the Volkswagen Model.

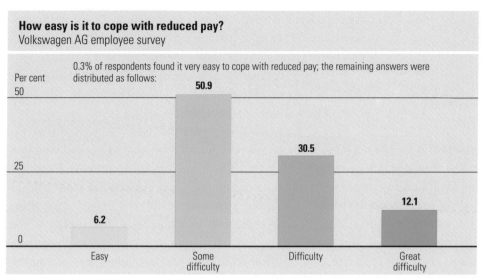

How easy is it to cope with reduced pay?
Volkswagen AG employee survey

0.3% of respondents found it very easy to cope with reduced pay; the remaining answers were distributed as follows:

Per cent

Easy	Some difficulty	Difficulty	Great difficulty
6.2	50.9	30.5	12.1

Sociology Institute, University of Erlangen/WSI, Düsseldorf

It is clear from the results of the survey that the route taken by Volkswagen from 1994 onwards is increasingly regarded by the population at large as a suitable alternative policy for maintaining levels of employment – and also enjoys the support of Volkswagen employees. This provided a basis on which a strategy for the collective bargaining could be developed.

On the other hand, the experience gained with the 28.8-hour week and the situation of the company itself also had to be taken into account. The first eighteen months during which the 28.8-hour week was in operation provided the important insight that although the company's working time models for the most part contained a capacity buffer, this reserve could only be used in a flexible manner by resorting to overtime. This had to provide the starting point for the 1995 pay negotiations – the need to agree on a manageable, cost-effective and flexible framework which would meet the requirements of a breathing company.

Analysis of the real market position and competitive situation of the company – which provide the basis for its negotiating stance in collective bargaining – showed that both the current agreements to safeguard employment and the accompanying measures by the company had contributed to an upswing in the company's fortunes. But a critical assessment also led to the conclusion that Volkswagen had only gone about 20% of the way towards turning the company around and achieving success.

To achieve further consolidation, it will be necessary to introduce further productivity gains and increases in efficiency. New products which Volkswagen brings on to the market over the next few years will have to be produced and marketed within shorter time-spans and with lower costs. The measures being rapidly introduced by the company – particularly its platform and sourcing strategies – will only become fully effective with new products. For this reason it was clear that employment levels would have to be further reduced in the medium-term and that this would mean the loss of further jobs at Volkswagen over the next two years. The dramatic aspect of this was that the scenario was already based on the assumption that the 28.8-hour week would be continued. In these circumstances, the scope for any concessions during the new round of collective bargaining was zero. A characteristic of this round, in comparison to 1993, was that from the very outset discussion focused on two specific points: increasing wages and safeguarding jobs.

It would have been wrong to claim that the structural crisis had been overcome or solved – the company's competitive disadvantages are still too great, demand too weak, the risks to entire markets from currency fluctuations too high, and profits too low.

The collective agreements were not due to run out until 31 July 1995 and could be terminated at that point with one month's notice. In advance of the negotiating round it was already clear that IG Metall would terminate the agreements, not least because of what – from its point of view – were regarded as "successful" wage rounds in the engineering and electrical industries that spring. Pay developments at Volkswagen over the previous three years also supported this assumption. In 1994 the parties to the collective agreement had held pay negotiations and agreed a 1% pay rise to come into effect on 1 August 1994, but real incomes had remained the same, since a 1% bonus agreed in connection with the 4-day week in the form of an "Advance from the '94 Round" no longer applied.

If the reduction of income connected with the introduction of the 4-day week is left out of consideration, then the point of departure for negotiations was this: the last pay increase at Volkswagen had taken place in November 1992 – i.e. almost three years previously. And during the intervening period the monthly gross income of employees had not changed.

In fact, if the changes in national insurance contributions from 1993 onwards (rise in contributions threshold, changes in rates, introduction of care insurance) and the so-called "solidarity levy" to help reconstruction in eastern Germany are taken into account, then the net monthly income of a married blue-collar worker had actually decreased by approximately 3.25% and that of a married white-collar worker by 4.5% between January 1993 and January 1995, the corresponding rates for a single person being about 4.5% and 6.2% respectively.

In view of this development, it was therefore clear to everyone involved that the metalworkers' union IG Metall – and the workforce – would make the question of wages one of their priorities. This had, incidentally, already been announced in the 1994 pay round.

The other aspect on which the negotiations focused was a continuation, renewal and extension of the agreement on safeguarding jobs. The agreements on safeguarding company locations and employment were, in fact, to stay in force at least until 31 December 1995 and could only be terminated thereafter with three month's notice. But at the suggestion of the company an early understanding was reached with the union that both issues should be negotiated together in the 1995 pay round. There were several reasons for this: on the one hand the question of safeguarding employment was also a high priority for the company, not least because of evidence of a continuing employment problem, as mentioned above.

Against this complex background one thing soon became very clear indeed: Volkswagen faced a "make-or-break" situation with the 1995 round of negotiations that could only be resolved in the context of a a complete package.

On the other hand, the 1993 agreement contained cost elements (i.e. the so-called "VW contribution" = Allowance 3) and consequential costs (so-called residual costs) resulting from the employment of 20,000 people, which had to be considered as a burden on the company in the outcome of the collective bargaining.

Beyond this it was clear that further adjustment measures served the purpose of safeguarding company locations and therefore employment – but also had cost implications. The money required for this was not available from redistribution either, and thus had to be found elsewhere.

The negotiations could only be successful if the elements in the overall package could be dealt with on the basis that they were interconnected. This, however, assumed a corresponding willingness amongst the parties involved to engage in genuine negotiations, and an understanding of the roles they had to play in this context. Otherwise the company and the union would race towards one another like two express trains on the same track and would inevitably collide.

The Volkswagen concept: initiating performance – creating security

In order to prevent such a total collision, Volkswagen developed a comprehensive concept, the basic characteristic of which was a firm intention to make work and pay at Volkswagen AG plants more secure. Competitiveness, safeguarding company locations and social responsibility were the clear reference points for the scenario. These served as the basis for formulating programmatic statements which provided the common thread running through the whole of the Volkswagen concept. They can be summarised as follows:

Programme for safeguarding employment, number 1:

- "Competitiveness on a global scale – every car is to reach the customer within 14 days."
- The customer rules, not the company: the customer's calculations have to tally – in the truest sense of the word.
- However attractive a product may be, if a company is judged to be "worse, slower and more expensive than others", this means that the calculation does not tally.
- Lost customers must be a thing of the past – this is the Volkswagen standard.

In order to achieve this, Volkswagen needed to further develop the 28.8-hour week into the Volkswagen Week.

LEISTUNG 🆆 **SICHERHEIT**
AUSLÖSEN 🆆 **EINLÖSEN**

TARIFRUNDE 95

Programme for safeguarding employment, number 2:

- "Locate in Germany – no permanent widening of the cost gap"
- Volkswagen is determined to develop and build cars in Germany, and that is precisely why we cannot ignore the fact that the gap in labour costs in relation to other parts of Europe – let alone the world – is so great that it will prove difficult to reduce.
- The competitive position of company locations in Germany must not be allowed to continue to deteriorate – the trend must be reversed.
- Volkswagen needs improvements particularly in the field of productivity. These can be reasonably achieved through further developments in collective agreements without having "to dip one's fingers into the pockets of the employees".

Programme for maintaining employment, number 3:

- "Continuation and renewal of the route Volkswagen has already taken."
- Volkswagen is aware of its regional importance as an employer and its social function and responsibilities as a major company.
- If the company is to take its social responsibilities seriously and continue to safeguard jobs, then all those concerned have to make a contribution – within the framework of what is acceptable.

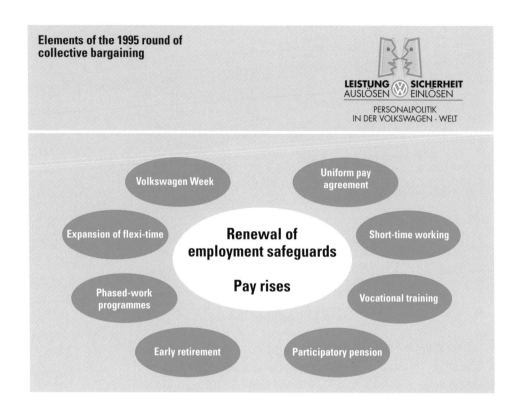

Elements of the 1995 round of collective bargaining

LEISTUNG AUSLÖSEN — SICHERHEIT EINLÖSEN

PERSONALPOLITIK IN DER VOLKSWAGEN - WELT

Volkswagen Week

Uniform pay agreement

Expansion of flexi-time

Renewal of employment safeguards

Pay rises

Short-time working

Phased-work programmes

Vocational training

Early retirement

Participatory pension

- This applies in particular to the need to progress further along the route taken by Volkswagen in 1993 – by further extending the guarantee of employment.

For these reasons and in view of the sheer complexity of the overall concept required, the company worked "as a team" to prepare for the negotiations. The overall concept, with its focus on "securing jobs" and "pay rises" was made up of a total of eight areas. The company was convinced that an open-minded and responsible approach to negotiations in all these would make it possible to reach agreement on the continued maintenance of job security and an appropriate pay rise.

The individual areas partly involved the further development of existing agreements (i.e. the Volkswagen Week and an expansion of flexi-time), but partly also the introduction of innovations in human resources policy which existed in 1993 only in theory or in rough outline, but which had since then been developed into negotiable building blocks (i.e. progressive work reduction programmes for older employees and participatory pensions).

The negotiations

The official round of negotiations started with IG Metall terminating the existing collective agreements by the deadline set. In its termination letter, IG Metall stated its agreement "to link negotiations on pay and job security" and declared its willingness "to fully include the agreements on safeguarding company locations and employment at Volkswagen in the negotiations for the 1995 pay round starting in August – without the need specifically to terminate those agreements".

The termination was linked with the following demands:

- 1. A 6% increase in wages and salaries to run for twelve months from 1 August 1995
- 2. A rise in the apprentice allowance from 1 August 1995
  Linkage to pay level F:
  in the first year of apprenticeship: 37%
  in the second year of apprenticeship: 37.5%
  in the third year of apprenticeship: 38.5%
  in the fourth year of apprenticeship: 40.5%
  Duration: 12 months
- 3. Extension of the agreement on the capital formation scheme for five years from 1 January 1995
- 4. Extension of the agreement on employment security

The negotiations began on 9 August immediately after the company shut down. The first negotiating session was followed by weekly rounds – some of them spread over two days – until a result was achieved in the sixth round on 11 and 12 September.

Besides a justification of its demands by IG Metall and a presentation by the VW wages commission of the economic factors affecting conditions in general and the company in particular, the first session was marked in particular by the presentation and detailed explanation of the Volkswagen pay concept "Initiating performance – creating security". This probably unique example of an employer entering the negotiations – not with a list of taboo subjects and exclusions, but on the offensive with an internally consistent proposal, clearly put the IG Metall into a position they were not familiar with.

Thus their first reaction was low-key, but positive: "VW presents list of topics: no offer – but a first step. On the plus side, VW wants to continue the system of safeguarding employment, but it is also clear that the conditions for employees have to be right" (in the words of the union publication Metall-Nachrichten, No. 4 of 14 August 1995). The approach taken by the company meant that at the start of the second session, IG Metall in turn felt obliged to present and explain the areas which it considered should form part of the "comprehensive system for safeguarding employment". It emerged that the areas set out by the two sides were in many respects identical.

But it soon emerged in the course of the negotiations that the underlying strategies of the negotiating partners in their search for a solution were in some cases quite contradictory and conflicting. This is, of course, in the nature of collective bargaining – at least as far as traditional roles are concerned. But it appears that

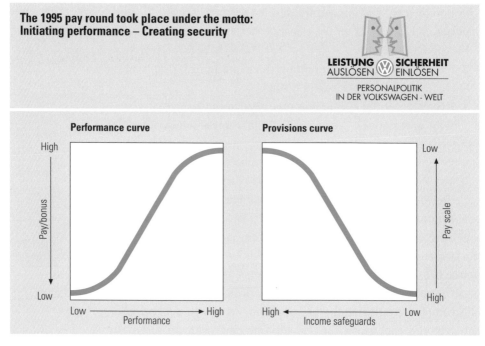

The 1995 pay round took place under the motto: Initiating performance – Creating security

LEISTUNG ⓦ SICHERHEIT
AUSLÖSEN   EINLÖSEN
PERSONALPOLITIK
IN DER VOLKSWAGEN - WELT

Performance curve

Provisions curve

it cannot be avoided even when the two parties engaged in negotiations are in agreement from the beginning that they will negotiate "openly" and concentrate on the issues at hand.

Of the numerous areas proposed by both sides there were some which quickly emerged in the course of the negotiations as capable of rapid solution – although always on condition that an overall settlement should also be reached. Included in these areas were "agreements to re-employ, short time working, progressive work reduction programmes for older employees" and agreement on "fixing the level of additional company pension contributions (participatory pensions)".

For most of the areas, however, the differences of opinion appeared to be insurmountable. The opposing positions emerged as soon as the negotiations began. The process of argumentation, negotiation, and of attempting to convince the other side permeated the talks right to the very end. The areas dealt with were essentially the following:

1. The duration and legal nature of a new agreement on maintaining company locations and jobs; this included the core subjects of the "28.8-hour week" and "Exclusion of mass dismissals by the company": IG Metall had demanded that as far as possible any agreement should be of unlimited duration or at least of considerably longer duration (than the present two years); it also demanded the abandonment of the 28.8-hour week as a special arrangement. This would have meant – from a legal perspective – that the 28.8-hour week would have become the normal working time and the so-called "shadow collective agreement", i.e. establishing the 35-hour week among other things, would have lapsed. For various reasons these demands were completely unacceptable to the company.

2. The requirements and conditions for including Saturdays in a flexible Volkswagen Week: In order to be able to implement Employment Programme Number 1 – "every car to reach the customer in 14 days" – which was an underlying element of the Volkswagen concept, the company had demanded the opportunity – subject to requirements and agreement at plant level – to be able to continue production on Saturdays if the relevant capacities were not available on other working days or had been exhausted.

Contrary to what was reported in the media, the company had not demanded that Saturday be made a regular working day. A limited number of Saturdays were simply to be used by the breathing company in the context of the flexibility pyramid and the Volkswagen Week, and the bonuses paid were to be reduced. The negotiations on this subject resulted in an acceptable compromise from the company's point of view.

3. The contribution of employees to the costs of safeguarding jobs: since the 1993 agreement on maintaining employment levels contained both cost elements for Volkswagen (so-called VW contribution = Allowance 3) as well as consequential costs (so-called residual costs), and since further staff adjustment measures were on the horizon which would also entail extra costs, the company had demanded a contribution from employees as part of the overall package.

This was not a question of "dipping into the pockets of the employees", but rather a sustained productivity increase, similar in kind and value, by all groups of employees: in the case of performance-based pay, through relinquishing paid breaks, and in the case of hourly-paid workers and salaried staff through corresponding cost-neutral increases in performance or longer working hours. Here, too, an acceptable compromise formula was achieved after long and tough negotiations.

4. Guaranteed employment for apprentices on completion of training: In the past, Volkswagen always trained above requirements, paid apprentices top wages, provided permanent employment for them without exception and was thus burdened with steadily increasing age-related costs at a time when its actual staff requirements were going down. The company therefore demanded among other things that the practice of providing permanent employment without exception should be relaxed and a permanent job should in future be made more dependent on proven suitability for the automobile industry being demonstrated during vocational training. This involved and socially controversial subject was allotted the importance it merited in the final collective agreement.

The agreement

During the night of 11 to 12 September 1995, agreement was finally achieved between the negotiating partners on the overall package for the '95 round of collective bargaining. 28 September 1995 was set as the date for both parties to announce

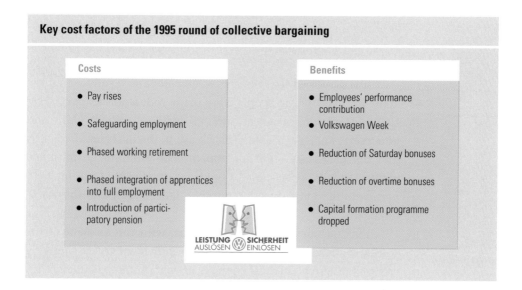

Key cost factors of the 1995 round of collective bargaining

Costs	Benefits
• Pay rises	• Employees' performance contribution
• Safeguarding employment	• Volkswagen Week
• Phased working retirement	• Reduction of Saturday bonuses
• Phased integration of apprentices into full employment	• Reduction of overtime bonuses
• Introduction of participatory pension	• Capital formation programme dropped

LEISTUNG AUSLÖSEN · SICHERHEIT EINLÖSEN

their acceptance of the outcome of the negotiations – and both parties met this deadline. All elements of the Volkswagen concept "Initiating performance – creating security" were included in the agreement.

Since the 1995 agreement between Volkswagen and the IG Metall – and the similar follow-up agreements with the other trade unions represented in the company, Deutsche Angestellten Gewerkschaft (DAG) and Christliche Gewerkschaft Metall (CGM) – is made up of numerous individual new regulations, the current new conditions in force at Volkswagen from January 1996 onwards will be set out below. The main focus of the agreement is a continuation of the system for safeguarding employment which began in 1994.

No mass dismissals by the company

In order to safeguard jobs the 28.8-hour week has continued to apply from 1 January 1996 onwards. This is tied, as before, to a basic condition in the collective agreement that there will be no layoffs. In contrast to the previous agreement, which went no further than to state that "there will be no company mass dismissals for the duration of the agreement", the new agreement, as well as defining the exclusion in principle of any mass workforce reductions by the company, also lays down the permitted exceptions to this rule.

It was agreed that the rule of no company layoffs would not apply in cases where people were made redundant as part of socially acceptable measures such as early retirement plans and other severance payments. This clause in the agreement ensures that the necessary staff adjustments can continue to be made within the legal provisions in the most practicable form for both parties to the employment contract – Volkswagen and the workforce.

Furthermore, it was agreed that, with the consent of the works council, the company could in individual cases change a contract of employment if changes in operational parameters required this. This clause in particular ensures that the required manpower flexibility and mobility, which is so closely connected with the policy to safeguard employment, is guaranteed. Experience with this has been gathered since 1994. Since the manpower surpluses – which in late 1993 were the driving force behind the first agreement of December 1993 to safeguard employment – were not distributed evenly over the six plants, bottlenecks had to be resolved through secondments and transfers. This affected the commercial vehicle plant in Hanover in particular, which temporarily suffered a considerable manpower shortage due to increased customer demand.

Such secondments and transfers meant that, from late 1994 onwards, approximately 1,240 employees from the Wolfsburg, Salzgitter, Emden and Brunswick plants were working in Hanover; 550 of these were apprentices who were offered employment by the company in Hanover at the end of their vocational training. Experience has shown that there are often problems connected with transfers of this sort, but these cannot be avoided if a system of safeguarding employment is to be introduced and sustained in the first place. This is the reason why a framework of flexibility and mobility is necessary – which includes – as a last resort, as it were – the legal instrument of being able to terminate a contract of employment if operational changes require this. Even if one is reluctant to use such an instrument, it should not be excluded from the outset.

The nature of the employment safeguards

Important aspects of the agreement to maintain levels of employment were, of course, its duration as well as the collective bargaining element. Both these aspects are of primary importance because the agreements to maintain levels of employment, old and new, are linked with the formal exclusion of any reductions of the workforce by the company. Moreover, the issuing of contractual employment guarantees has to be considered and balanced very carefully – particularly at the present time – and may only be seriously considered for a clearly defined and predictable period. There are clear contractual conditions involved. The new agreement on safeguarding jobs came into force on 1 January 1996 and may be "terminated with three months' notice to the end of the year, at the earliest on 31 December 1997".

Furthermore, as well as the undertaking to start negotiations on a follow-on settlement immediately if the present one is terminated, the parties to the agreement set out the following provision in § 7.3 of the new agreement on safeguarding jobs: "If there is no agreement (through a follow-up settlement), this collective agreement expires six months after the agreement has lapsed, at the earliest on 30 June 1998. In this case the normal provisions of the collective agreements (including Section 4.1 of this agreement) will apply in their then valid form".

This provision on the duration of the agreement ensures that from a legal point of view the new agreement on safeguarding jobs initially represents a long-term settlement. Unlike a fixed-term agreement which, as a rule, is only valid for a specified period, because in the first instance, the agreement itself does not contain a specific expiry date. Its termination is dependent on one of the contractual parties taking action, to terminate it.

But it is plain from the possibility that the agreement may be terminated, and specifically from the clause according to which the conditions of the ordinary pay settlement come into force again if there is no follow-up settlement, that from a legal perspective the agreement to safeguard jobs is actually no ordinary permanent agreement. On the contrary, it represents a collective agreement with special working time and payment provisions which may be dissolved and on which notice may be given. If in doubt, it may be terminated unilaterally by either side and is thus of limited duration in the widest sense of the word. The special nature of the new agreement to safeguard jobs in relation to "normal" pay settlements is also evident in § 6. According to this, the provisions of the other pay agreements continue to apply in so far as no other provisions are laid down in this agreement. Otherwise the legal form and quality chosen for the new agreement corresponds to the preceding agreement of 1993.

Here too the company and the union had agreed – even if on the basis of different time scales – that after coming into force the accord could be terminated with three months' notice to the end of the year, but not before 31 December 1995, and that the ordinary regulations would come into force again six months after the end of the agreement if no follow-up agreement had been negotiated between the parties in the intervening period.

Thus the new agreement on maintaining levels of employment contains special working time and pay provisions just like the previous one, and combines these with a contractual guarantee of employment for a limited and justifiable period of two and a half years. Depending on future developments, the form of agreement selected offers both parties the option to make an appropriate joint decision in 1997, taking into account the conditions prevailing at the time.

The Volkswagen Week: a further development of the 4-day week

The introduction of the 4-day week in January 1994 was a solution born of necessity. Given continuing concern about unemployment, together with an effective working time (including overtime) of 28.8 hours in VW's six plants in western Germany in 1994, the courageous and unconventional decision of December 1993 turned out to be a step in the right direction. At the same time, after the collective agreement was implemented in the plants, it quickly became evident that it was beginning to come up against its limits. Against this background and in view of the fact that the automobile industry is subject to seasonal demand fluctuations, it became clear that the 28.8-hour week would need to be developed further.

A company that was so dependent on the market had to set itself a 14-day delivery target for every customer in order to survive against global competition. The 4-day week, with the greater flexibility it already offered, also had to be used to full advantage within the package of collectively negotiated measures.

That is how the Volkswagen Week came about. In a breathing company the working week is determined by the volume of orders received. The crucial element here is to develop an ongoing, breathing working time which offers the flexibility to set priorities according to customer requirements. The Volkswagen Week thus becomes predictable, all arbitrary elements having been removed. Its core is the 28.8-hour week, but what is new is the "flexibility cascade", which provides the basis for plant-level decisions on fixing working hours according to a strict order of priorities.

The sequence of priorities consists of five stages: only when flexibility in hours per day (first priority) has been exhausted is the step taken towards the less popular daily shifts (second priority). Only when these have been exhausted is the further step taken to invoke flexibility in terms of days (third priority). Only when working days from Monday to Friday have been exhausted is there a move towards less popular Saturday working (fourth priority). And when all these stages have been exhausted the last priority is brought into play – flexibility in manufacturing location, with production volume being transferred to another plant (fifth priority).

As laid down in the collective agreement, the Volkswagen Week is utilised above all in production and production-dependent areas. But by plant-based agreement it may be implemented in other areas as well. In principle, the weekly working hours are distributed over four or five working days (from Monday to Friday

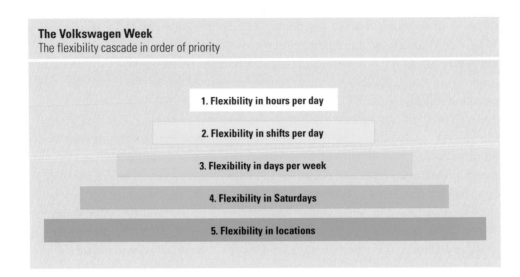

The Volkswagen Week
The flexibility cascade in order of priority

1. Flexibility in hours per day

2. Flexibility in shifts per day

3. Flexibility in days per week

4. Flexibility in Saturdays

5. Flexibility in locations

as a rule) by means of a shift plan and in agreement with workforce representatives. This was already being done in the past, although with one disadvantage: the shift plans remained constant over the whole year. The only way to deviate from them – in the case of increased demand for instance – was by means of overtime. With the advent of the 4-day week at Volkswagen, overtime was no longer a cost factor, as bonuses only applied from the 36th hour per week onwards. But as a rule overtime was dependent on the agreement of the works council in each individual case and could thus not be used at short notice in a large organisation in order to allow it to breathe with the ebb and flow of demand.

Under the new agreement on safeguarding employment, it is now possible, within the framework of the annual programme and working time plan, to distribute weekly working hours irregularly over the year and thus adapt them to the volume of orders. Under the Volkswagen Week, working hours may be extended up to eight hours per day and 38.8 hours per week without resulting in overtime payments. And if this time is insufficient to build the customer his car, the Volkswagen Week makes it possible to agree with the local works council that Saturday working will be included in the plan for the year.

Beyond this, the possibility remains, of course – particularly when demand peaks at short notice – to agree with the works council to run additional shifts over the course of the year. In this context, new regulations on Saturday and overtime working have been introduced. The additional rate for Saturday and overtime working (from the 36th hour/week onwards) has been set at a uniform 30%, whereas in the past a supplement of 50% was paid for Saturday working and 40% for overtime from Monday to Friday (Saturday working incorporated into the shift plan – in a fully continuous shift system for instance – remains at the 50% supplement on Saturdays).

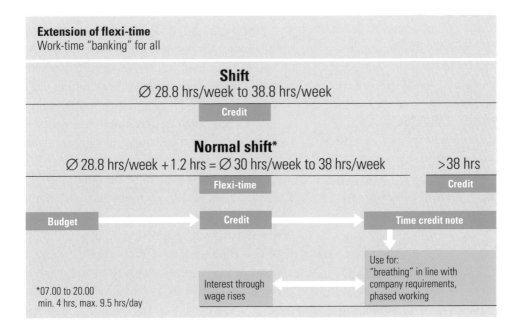

The monthly wage does not change, even when working hours within the framework of the Volkswagen Week are irregular – irrespective of whether a greater or lesser amount of work is carried out in response to fluctuations in orders. The basis is provided by the 28.8-hours per week, adhered to as an average over the whole year. In order to make this "work time banking " operate successfully, the collective agreement allows for the establishment of individual working time accounts which record credits and debits for the purpose of later settlement. Any deviations from the annual plan – for example as a result of changes in incoming orders – take place with the agreement of the works council and have to be communicated to the staff affected two months prior to the event.

A bold innovation: individual responsibility for working hours

An empowered workforce is more important than ever for the success of the company. This is demonstrated very clearly in those processes in which employees are allowed to participate and make their own contribution. Examples of this are the 14,000 or more CIP[2] workshops and new forms of work organisation such as group, team and project work. Hence the expectation contained in the M4 profile that employees should be involved in determining their own work.

The Volkswagen Week enables the company to breathe in response to market demand. It allows a degree of working time flexibility at virtually no extra cost and thus contributes to safeguarding company locations and employment levels. The Volkswagen Week brings us significantly closer to our customers.

VW's approach to participation involves a high degree of trust between the company and its employees. This will, necessarily, replace the control from above which for decades was traditionally exercised in many areas. For example, a company and workforce oriented towards processes and value-added activities cannot at the same time maintain a rigid system of timekeeping, using a time clock. In the context of the changes we were introducing, it was only logical to build on individual responsibility and trust amongst our employees and complete the long-overdue paradigm change from clocking on and off to concentrating on functions and process requirements – from timekeeping to individual time autonomy.

Tasks and processes are controlled more effectively by agreeing on goals than by operating a clocking-on system. Individual responsibility for working hours has now become an essential element throughout the Volkswagen World. The 1995 round of collective bargaining offered an opportunity to take a fresh look at flexi-time arrangements and adapt them to new circumstances and challenges. The parties involved were in agreement that any expansion of flexi-time to improve competitiveness and safeguard locations of company operations and employment levels required a more flexible working time framework.

Keeping customer requirements and deadlines in mind, this working time framework is filled in by agreement between each employee and his superior, taking into account company requirements (i.e. tasks and processes) and the personal interests of the employee. Here too – as in shift work during 1995 – the time clock was abolished.

What is good for management is also good for each employee – and the workforce as a whole. If Volkswagen considers its managers responsible enough to determine their working hours, then it should allow the entire workforce to do the same!

The fixing of core hours – where necessary – is delegated to shop-floor level, where it can be carried out in a customer-friendly way, taking account of individual requirements. The working time framework extends to a maximum of 13 hours per day and – together with distribution over the week, the start and finish of the flexi-time framework and, where relevant, the fixing of core working time – is laid down in plant-level agreements.

Within the framework of this arrangement, employees can independently determine, according to the number of orders, the start and finishing times of their working day. Daily working time consists of a minimum of 4 and a maximum of 9.5 hours. The ad-

Flexi-time
Major change in the results of the 1995 collective bargaining agreement compared with 1993

	Old	New
Working time	28.8-hour week as annual average	28.8-hour week as annual average + 1.2 hrs performance contribution per week
Target working hours **4-day week** **5-day week**	7.2 hrs 5.76 hrs	7.5 hrs 6 hrs
Control of working hours	Time clock card	Company no longer records
Working hours (minimum)	5 hrs 48 mins	4 hrs
Working hours (maximum)	9.5 hrs	9.5 hrs within the time framework of 13 hrs (07.00-20.00)

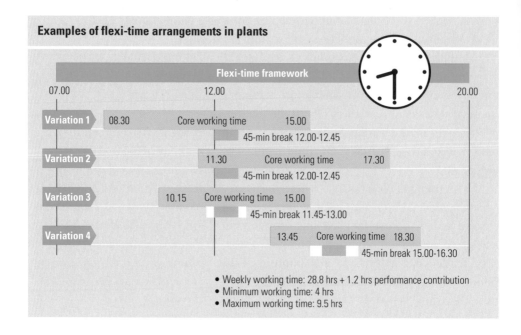

Examples of flexi-time arrangements in plants

Flexi-time framework

07.00   12.00   20.00

Variation 1   08.30   Core working time   15.00
45-min break 12.00-12.45

Variation 2   11.30   Core working time   17.30
45-min break 12.00-12.45

Variation 3   10.15   Core working time   15.00
45-min break 11.45-13.00

Variation 4   13.45   Core working time   18.30
45-min break 15.00-16.30

- Weekly working time: 28.8 hrs + 1.2 hrs performance contribution
- Minimum working time: 4 hrs
- Maximum working time: 9.5 hrs

ditional performance contribution agreed on for the indirect sector means that, after the 30th hour per week, any additional hours worked qualify for time compensation. Thus – while still allowing for customer requirements – every employee operates within the Volkswagen Week with a high degree of freedom.

The time credit note

Even with the most precise planning, businesses which operate globally and have international manufacturing operations are inevitably subject to circumstances beyond their control. Unexpected sales opportunities, development contracts, supply projects – and also bottlenecks and similar problems – can all mean that planned working hours have to be abandoned. When all other possibilities have been exhausted, the only way to create additional capacity and meet the customer's requirements is to resort to overtime – that is, a volume of work which departs from the average annual working time.

The basic principle which operates at Volkswagen is that any overtime worked is reimbursed in the form of paid time off, and the collective agreement makes provision for payment only in ex-

The Time credit note

ceptional circumstances agreed with the workforce representatives at plant level. Furthermore, the parties to the collective agreement have to be informed of this in advance in order to avoid abuse of the system. In principle, overtime should be taken in paid leave – and this is new – within twelve months (under the old collective agreement the period was six months). But it is possible to take paid time off for overtime beyond this period, provided the employee and his supervisor have agreed on this. The collective agreement here speaks of "taking time off for a specified purpose".

The collective agreement expressly refers to the "Volkswagen time credit note" as the method for reimbursing overtime in the form of paid time off. This is a "time" bill-of-exchange, with interest paid in the form of an increase in rates. If time off is taken with the "Volkswagen time credit note", the current value at the time the leave is taken forms the basis on which the monthly remuneration is based. This also applies to credit notes issued in previous years, thus ensuring that the time credit note does not suffer any loss of value.

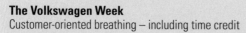

The Volkswagen Week
Customer-oriented breathing – including time credit

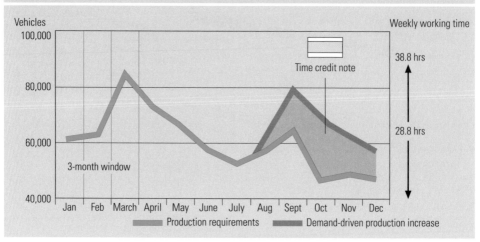

Details concerning the time credit note are agreed at plant level, although the minimum content is laid down in the collective agreement. The procedure is as follows:

- Overtime may only be arranged within the framework of the approved budget.
- Every superior receives a kind of cheque book containing time credit notes on the basis of the approved budget.
- The superior issues a credit note for time off accrued as the result of overtime worked. This records the accrued time off, and is simultaneously recorded in an individual time account.
- Time off may be taken in various ways, for example for a specific purpose, which can include longer breaks and block times – for example for training, house-building, long vacation trips and similar reasons. The time credit may also be used for reducing working hours during the transition to retirement or for an additional reduction in working hours within the framework of the phased working programme for older employees.
- The "cashing in" of time credit notes for a specific purpose is discussed by the employee with his superior. An agreement reached by this means is binding on the company and the employee. In order to allow the company to plan ahead effectively

and coherently, time off taken for specific purposes has to be applied for according to its length – up to four weeks' leave requires one month's notice, between four weeks' and three months' requires three months', and anyone planning to take more than three months off must apply six months in advance.

The time credit note thus makes it possible to accrue rights to time off for a wide variety of possible reasons. Unavoidable overtime today thus provides security of employment for the future.

Contribution by the workforce to safeguarding employment

Continuation of the policy of safeguarding employment at Volkswagen was contingent upon the workforce making a contribution. The collective agreement contains two elements in this regard: one for the direct sector, i.e. those on performance-based pay; and one for the indirect sector, i.e. those on hourly rates and pay. In both cases the intended effect is the same: from 1 January 1996 all those on hourly rates and white-collar office staff must work 1.2 hours more for the same pay. For those on performance-based pay, the corresponding increase in performance is achieved from the same date through a 50% reduction in the current five-minute paid rest period to a maximum of two-and-a-half minutes per hour.

Workforce performance contribution	
Employees in production sector	**Staff in indirect areas**
● Reduction in breaks	● Additional time 1.2 hrs/week
● Breaks credited	● Autonomy in organising own time
● Manpower levels based on competitiveness	● Tasks and function-related agreement on targets

For the indirect sector, the company and union have agreed that the additional weekly performance contribution of 1.2 hours can be achieved by various means. The relevant section of the collective agreement offers both parties a number of options for finding the appropriate solution for each of the various working time models. The agreement outlines the following possibilities in a list intended to be illustrative rather than exhaustive:

- The extra input is calculated within the framework of flexi-time; for instance, the daily quota of working hours calculated on the basis of a 28.8-hour week at 7.2 hours or 7 hours and 12 minutes (for a four-day week) is extended by 18 minutes to 7.5 hours.
- The extra input takes the form of additional working days – for instance in the case of a 4-day week one additional day is worked over a period of six weeks (= 24 working days).
- Deduction of days off work. This alternative is possible in connection with all working time models in which the difference between the working time laid down in the shift plan and the working time laid down in the collective agreement is made up by days off work (so-called free shifts). This is practised throughout the company in instances where there are fully continuous shift operations as well as in normal three-shift operations.
- Inclusion in overtime calculations.

In the direct sector the additional input is achieved – as already indicated – by a reorganisation of the breaks and rest periods contained in the collective agreement. The basis for this is provided in the "Agreement on Basic Conditions" which was also concluded in conjunction with the 1995 collective agreement. It contains two regulatory strands – on the one hand, the requirements and procedures relating to performance monitoring and personnel assessment for hourly paid employees and, on the other, the new arrangements concerning breaks and rest periods for those on performance-related pay – which constitute a special provision superseding the provisions currently in force in the collective agreement on basic wage conditions ("LORA"). In this context there was some uncertainty and confusion at shop-floor level immediately after the collective agreement was concluded. But the text of the agreement makes it quite clear that this is what is intended: according to § 4, provisions on basic wage conditions in the preceding collective agreement continue to apply in so far as they do not contradict the new agreement. But this in turn implies that if there are specific arrangements on basic wage conditions in the new agreement, the "LORA" collective agreement will not apply.

There was agreement among the parties to the collective agreement that "LORA", with its detailed and complicated provisions, required a comprehensive reworking. This will be tackled separately by the parties, but the key points concerning payment methods should be reorganised immediately in order to make it easier to increase productivity. This applies in particular to the new agreement on personal breaks and rest periods. It came into force on 1 January 1996 and provides for adequate account to be taken of personal breaks and rest periods within the framework of the agreement on manpower assessment or workload. Here local conditions are of crucial importance. The question of what length of personal breaks and rest periods is appropriate in the context of the agreement has to be negotiated with the works council. If there is no agreement, then a personal break of three minutes per hour and a paid rest period of two-and-a-half minutes per hour is to be implemented. The result of this is that in the case of a failure to agree, the personal break remains unchanged while the paid rest period is reduced by 50%.

But a corresponding arrangement in relation to rest periods also applies to another situation: if a longer rest period – in specific terms, up to five minutes – should be necessary, then only two-and-a-half minutes of it are to be paid from 1 January 1996 onwards. Any requirement for rest periods over and above that is regarded as unpaid time off. The agreement further envisages that periods and activities which represent a change of workload in contrast to work on the production line, and as such constitute a relief from normal work (i.e. supervisory and control functions, materials transport and preparation, as well as waiting periods as the result of process times for example) should be added to the rest period. A similar provision is made for interruptions (e.g. because of technical faults, logistical problems/shortage of materials, quality problems, maintenance work, etc.) if they last for more than five minutes.

Finally, these new arrangements for personal breaks and rest periods take account of positive developments which have now led to more humane working conditions through the consistent development of technology and work-organisation methods. The result of the new structure has been an overall reduction in paid rest periods by 50% and the sanctioning – depending on the local situation – of the addition of work periods and interruptions constituting a relief from normal work to the remaining 2.5-minute rest period per hour. The new arrangement of personal breaks and rest periods is embedded in a new system of performance and personnel assessment according to which workload and assessment within the framework of performance-related pay will in future be agreed between the company and the works council on the basis of planning and reference data. This also applies to changes which occur as a result of the ongoing process of improvement.

In the case of hourly rates – which hitherto fell outside the wage agreement – the agreement on wage conditions stipulates that performance and performance targets are to be agreed in discussions between the employee and his superior. The "Agreement on Wage Conditions" as a whole represents a reaction to a changed economic situation and working conditions. It contains one short-term effect – the adjustment of the rest periods means a productivity increase of approximately 4.2% for the company – and contains a framework necessary for achieving further productivity increases and improving competitiveness in the medium term.

The implementation of the agreement as a whole – and of personal assessment in particular – will require a great deal of commitment, as it calls for a fundamental change in thinking. It requires a methodical approach, going through the plants step-by-step and making the relevant decisions together with the works council after a precise analysis of local conditions. The continuation of the 28.8-hour week, the inclusion in the collective agreement of the Volkswagen Week, the agreement on performance targets in the indirect sector and the new arrangements for personal breaks and rest periods led to a need for immediate action on 1 January 1996. Arrangements for plant working times and breaks had to be re-thought.

Every working time model requires agreements on the necessary adjustments between the plant management and the works council. In principle both parties were able to use existing working time models as a guide, for the agreement of 28 September 1995 regarding the safeguarding of locations of company operations and employment lays down as a principle for working time distribution that the weekly working time – 28.8 hours averaged over the year – may be spread in shifts over either four or five working days. This clause in the agreement meant, incidentally, that the parties to the agreement had taken the real situation into account. Although the earlier agreement prescribed a 4-day week as the basic working period, only permitting a 5-day week under exceptional circumstances subject to the agreement of both parties, production and organisational requirements meant that the latter arrangement – a 5-day week with shorter daily working hours – had to be invoked for approximately 25,000 employees, particularly in the Wolfsburg plant. Beyond this, the working time models had – and still have – to be developed further into a flexible Volkswagen Week.

Collective agreement on short time working

The policy on safeguarding employment as pursued by Volkswagen since 1994 and renewed now for at least a further two years requires supplementary human resources measures. As early as 1994, the parties to the collective bargaining had concluded agreements on "Phased Integration of Apprentices into Full Employment after Training" and "Work-free Block Time".

Both agreements were also included in the 1995 collective bargaining round.

The agreement on work-free block time was continued without any substantial changes. The parties to the collective settlement agreed that the instrument of short time working as allowed by law can make a substantial supplementary contribution towards safeguarding employment. This instrument is therefore to be used when required, within the permissible legal framework.

According to the agreement, the introduction of short time working is, as previously, possible when the required legal conditions – i.e. economic or structural reasons – prevail. In such a situation, for the whole short time working period Volkswagen pays – again as previously – a supplement to statutory short time pay which is structured degressively for the various levels of wage and salary grades and assures employees an average of 85% of their normal monthly income.

A new element in this connection was the agreement that these degressive supplementary payments would be applied from 1 January 1996 to all matters related to short time working. It replaced the previous arrangement contained in the skeleton collective agreement whereby a supplement was paid for normal (usually cyclically determined) short time working which guaranteed employees 95% of their monthly income – restricted to a maximum of ten short time working days per month.

Phased Integration of Apprentices into Full Employment after Training

In the new agreement the "Phased Integration of Apprentices into Full Employment after Training" was also continued essentially unchanged, as it had proved its value as a supplementary instrument. On the basis of this agreement, apprentices successfully concluding their final examinations are offered employment and are gradually integrated into full-time employment by steadily increasing part-time work: over the first two years this comprises 20 hours per week, rising to 24 hours per week over the following eighteen months. A freshly trained apprentice is thus entitled to a contract of full-time employment after three-and-a-half years.

Beyond this, it is possible under the agreement for the plant management and works council to deviate from this progression if there is agreement that there is a shortage of personnel at the production location concerned. This clause enables the two parties to react flexibly to the personnel situation in their plants, for instance by shortening the stages of part-time working or – in extreme cases – agreeing to offer immediate full-time employment to the trainee. The latter is, however, only possible to a limited degree: it is only permitted under the agreement for a maximum period of one year.

Furthermore, the agreement also covers the prerequisites for mobility. Thus an offer of employment in another plant fulfils the conditions set out in the agreement if the criteria and principles which apply to all employees mean that the individual concerned can be reasonably expected to accept it. If this is the case, then that individual is obliged to accept the offer of employment and will not be offered an alternative. In order to provide an incentive in such cases, the agreement allows the apprentice to be permanently exempted from phased short time working.

In this connection, the arrangements for the transition of apprentices into employment which had operated at Volkswagen for a good forty years were completely revised. This was one of the most controversial issues in the negotiations. The company's main motive in this respect was not that it was unwilling to continue to offer employment to apprentices in the future. On the contrary, the starting point was twofold: a determination to continue to increase the quality of training and apprentices by means of a continuous assessment procedure suggested by the company for the training process (suitability for the automotive industry); and also a desire to continue to offer high-quality vocational training through a combination of factors "apprenticeships – remuneration – employment – retirement provisions", at a reasonable and stable cost.

Under the agreement apprentices have a fundamental claim to employment after training. This does not apply, however, if there are important reasons to the contrary related to the performance or behaviour of an individual. A continuous assessment process during training was introduced as a supplementary measure. Six-monthly assessment of learning objectives and progress interviews were introduced on the basis of differentiated training criteria. Any recommendation that an apprentice be offered employment is based on the progress made by that individual in addition to the exam results.

Phased Working Programme for Older Employees

In addition to the existing "Phased Integration of Apprentices into Full Employment after Training" model, which supported the policy of safeguarding employment, the new agreement also introduced a "Phased Working Programme for Older Employees", thus realising an idea which had existed since 1993. By enabling older employees to progress in stages towards retirement, their jobs are gradually released for the progressive entry of young people into employment. Under the new agreement, staff at Volkswagen can, from 1 January 1996 onwards, make the transition to retirement via three stages of part-time working. The first stage provides for a working time of 24 hours per week, followed by 20 hours per week and finally 18 hours per week.

The new arrangements also demonstrate that early retirement or part-time working for older employees are not to be viewed in isolation. Together with the work time credit programme and participatory pensions, the phased working programme for older employees offers a new overall package for the transition to retirement.

During the period of transition to retirement the income of the person concerned is assured to a limited degree through a supplement which is paid by the company in addition to the part-time pay. This is calculated – as for short time working – according to a degressive acceptability curve, i.e. it is structured degressively according to the pay scales and guarantees employees an average of 85% of their previous full-time pay.

This progressive transition to retirement with its restricted safeguarding of income is designed to appeal to people who may prefer to have a longer transition period, for example for personal reasons. But it is also addressed to those whose expertise is at present indispensable for the company, for instance because it is required for special projects or needs to be passed on to younger colleagues over a longer transitional period.

The decision as to whether an employee may enter the programme can thus only be made in relation to the requirements and circumstances of the employer. As well as meeting the needs of the company this must, of course, also take into account the personal circumstances of the individual.

On this basis the "Phased Working Programme for Older Employees" involves the following: Individuals do not have an automatic right to take part in the progressive transition into retirement – the relevant decision has to be made by the company, in agreement with the works council, taking into account the needs of the company and the personal circumstances of the individual.

In view of imminent legislation on phased early retirement, the parties to the collective agreement only concluded a framework agreement, delegating the task of agreeing on further details of the new Volkswagen programme for part-time work for older employees (earliest possible entry age, duration of the various stages, etc.) to the two parties.

Guarantee of re-employment

In the course of the collective bargaining round, the two parties also discussed, from an employment policy perspective, an instrument which had already been agreed in 1990. From 1 January 1996, members of staff can request permission to leave the company for a period of up to five years. The precondition for approval is that there are no objections from the company's point of view. In such cases the individual involved receives a guarantee of re-employment in a job of a similar nature and status to their present one. In the past, staff were only able to leave employment for a set period under specific circumstances:

- to care for children and members of their family
- to bring up children – e.g. subsequent to statutory leave granted for this purpose
- to undergo further training

Thus, guaranteed re-employment was motivated in the past primarily by social policy considerations, but has now, as part of an evolving human resources policy, been extended to include the aspects of safeguarding employment and reducing costs – against a background of a new flexible definition of the relationship between employee and employer. Leaving employment with a guarantee of re-employment is now possible without one of the above reasons having to apply. This opens up opportunities for individuals which they may well have wished to make use of in the past but which were not available at the time.

As this measure also contributes in the widest sense to safeguarding employment, there is one thing which must, of course, be excluded. The guarantee of re-employment was – and continues to be – conditional upon no other work subject to social security contributions being undertaken on a freelance basis or for another employer during the leave period. If this should happen, then the guarantee of re-employment is no longer legally binding.

The option of leaving the company for a defined period of time – with a guarantee of full re-employment. It was the realisation of an option which for many must have seemed destined to remain a dream!

Such a stipulation is logical. The new option of leaving employment with a guarantee of re-employment and without having to provide any particular reason, gives the employee risk-free room for manoeuvre and allows the company to temporarily reduce personnel costs – thus helping to safeguard employment. What this instrument cannot do – and is not designed to do – is remove the element of risk to which employees leaving the company would normally be subjected through probationary periods with a new employer or through setting up their own business.

Common wage agreement

The round of collective bargaining was characterised overall by its focus on safeguarding employment levels and on increased pay. But the agreement also managed to take a step forward and achieve a change of emphasis in relation to qualitative aspects of wages policy.

The differentiation between white- and blue-collar workers has for some time been challenged and is increasingly losing its meaning – not just in legislative and legal terms. Parliament and the courts are increasingly unifying the legal provisions affecting white- and blue-collar workers (i.e. notice periods, law on sickness pay, etc.) or alternatively – particularly in the case of industrial tribunals – are in most cases declaring any surviving differential regulations as being illegal. The central argument on which industrial tribunals base their decision is the principle of equal treatment enshrined in labour law and the observation that the distinction between white- and blue-collar workers in itself does not provide any legal basis for accepting distinct regulations for the two groups.

If such a distinction is to be made, then the law stipulates that there has to be a comprehensible, reasonable and objective basis for it. This can be illustrated using the example of notice periods. In principle the law does not (any longer) recognise different notice periods for white- and blue-collar workers if – with the exception of the distinction between the two groups under labour law – there are no other objective differences. The courts have, for instance, recognised as an objective reason that an employer must react quickly to cyclical employment problems within his company, and must be able to make a distinction in this context. For this reason they have, amongst other things, declared shorter notice periods for employees working in production (as opposed to those employed in administration) to be legally permissible. This decision was based on the argument that cyclical employment problems usually have to be countered more rapidly in production than in the administration. The employer therefore had to be given this right. If it is the case – the line of legal argument continues – that it is almost exclusively blue-collar workers who are employed in production and white-collar workers who are employed in administration, then a distinction exists between the two groups – though this is based not on their status as employees but on a legally acceptable distinction between production and administrative workers.

The differentiation between blue- and white-collar workers is becoming irrelevant not only in law, but also in terms of day-to-day reality in the plants.

New techniques, technologies, and forms of work organisation – as well as the implementation of lean manufacturing and lean production strategies – require decisions to be made locally and make new demands on employees in terms of skills and the tasks they are required to carry out. This applies not only to the so-called administrative (i.e. white-collar) sector but equally – and increasingly – to production sectors. Activities, requirements and skills are converging between white- and blue-collar workers. This development has resulted over the last ten years or so in collective bargaining policy increasingly focusing on the question of "an agreement on uniform wage scales for blue- and white-collar workers". Such common wage scales already exist in some sec-

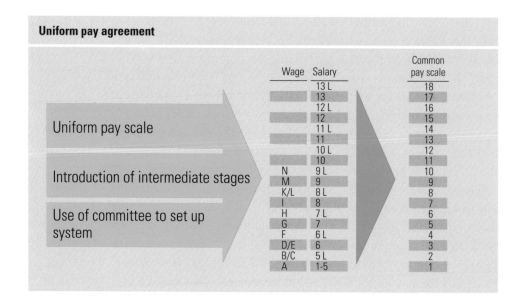

tors (e.g. the brewing and chemical industries) and are under negotiation in others (e.g. the engineering and electrical industries).

At Volkswagen, too, the two negotiating parties had already
taken a first step in this direction. In the 1991 round of collective
bargaining, both sides had agreed on an adjustment of the wage
and salary structure. Intermediate salary scales, so-called "L-
scales", were incorporated into the salary structure, and, in addition, the monthly amounts in the wage and salary groups were
unified to the extent that they applied to work of similar value.
Such an adjustment of the wage and salary structures meant that
the parties to the collective agreement had taken a first step and
created the necessary organisational preconditions for a joint pay
agreement for blue- and white-collar workers. Since then it has
not been possible to make any further progress in that field for
various reasons, although both parties had agreed on launching
negotiations on a joint pay agreement in the preamble to the 1991
collective agreement.

A further step has now been taken as a result of the 1995
round. It was agreed that from 1 January 1996 the currently sep-
arate monthly wage and salary tables would be merged and replaced by a pay table with uniform pay scales from 1 to 18. In

this connection it was also agreed that the current "L-scales" would be applied for the first time to white-collar workers. All white-collar workers receiving a bonus based on performance assessment under the current pay agreement were put on to the "L-scale" from 1 January 1996 and the performance-related bonus programme was abolished. Under the new agreement, white-collar workers who do not receive performance-related bonuses may be put on to the "L-scale" of their basic salary group after a maximum of two years.

Through the new agreement the "L-scales" have taken on the character of "experience-related scales". The individual performance and experience of white-collar workers can be taken into account through the different rates at which they progress up the scale and thus earn more than others who do not perform so well or are less experienced. The current arrangements are an interim solution which applies for a transitional phase. A unified pay agreement based on the principle of "work and pay assessment according to uniform criteria and procedures" still awaits realisation.

This task has been delegated to a commission made up of equal numbers of representatives of the management and the workforce. It will have to draw up an overall solution which is both acceptable as a just and modern method of organising pay and also takes into account cost considerations related to the need to remain competitive. Beyond that it has to unify regulations which are still distinct (i.e. those concerning the appointment of deputies, and the orientation phase after taking up a new post etc.). To carry out this task effectively will require detailed and time-consuming talks and negotiations.

Participatory pension plan

The other completely new qualitative aspect of the wage policy contained in the agreement is the participatory pension scheme which forms part of the overall package. There was no dispute between the parties over the advantages of an additional company contribution rather than other forms of provision. There was also agreement on the present gaps in provision and risks for the individual, due essentially to current statutory intervention

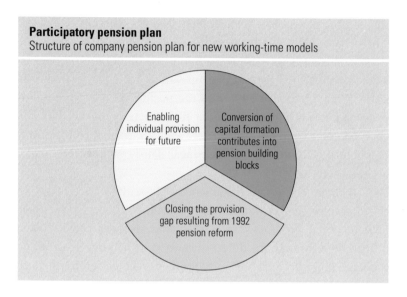

Participatory pension plan
Structure of company pension plan for new working-time models

Enabling individual provision for future

Conversion of capital formation contributes into pension building blocks

Closing the provision gap resulting from 1992 pension reform

(including the 1992 pensions reform law), and on the assessment that the trend towards further reductions in benefits is likely to continue.

The result was that it did not take long for both sides to agree that the introduction of additional company provisions was both justified and important. The only differences were over the way in which such a participatory pension plan should be financed. While the company considered the conversion of, for instance, 0.5% or 1% of the agreed pay rise from cash into pension provision to be a realistic target, IG Metall for its part declared that conversion of the employer's contribution to the capital formation plan was the only possible alternative. The relevant agreement ran out at the end of 1994 and its extension was subject to further negotiation. IG Metall stated that it was prepared to negotiate on the continuation of this pay agreement in the form of a supplementary provision. The condition, however, was that there should be agreement on an acceptable transitional arrangement which provided employees with an appropriate and reasonable continuation or termination of their current capital formation plans.

Against this background, the two parties agreed that the sum of DM 52 per month presently being paid by the company as its contribution to the capital formation plan should cease in principle from 1 January 1996 and be replaced by a contribution to a supplementary company pension based on actuarial principles. In contrast to the capital formation plan, the individual does not have any powers of disposition over the "pension capital". This is particularly important for the legal quality of the agreement within the meaning of the law on improving company pensions. An interim arrangement ensures that there will be no individual hardship during the transition from the capital formation plan to the participatory pension model. Thus every employee has the opportunity, for a maximum of one-and-a-half years, to continue with his current form of investment using the company contributions to the capital formation plan. Beyond this, proven cases of hardship may be exempted from the participatory pension plan for a further year. While exemption for the first one-and-a-half years merely requires an application from the individual, further exemption on grounds of hardship requires a positive decision from a commission made up of equal numbers of management and employees' representatives. As a result of this balanced transitional arrangement, the additional company pension contributions will come into full effect as a qualitatively new pay element from 1 July 1998 at the latest.

The participatory pension established under the new agreement is based on a building-block system. The benefits are available only in case of death, invalidity or when the statutory retirement age is reached.

1996 pay rise

The agreement on the areas contained in the overall package – safeguarding employment in particular – paved the way for an appropriate rise in wages and salaries. A monthly sum of DM 200 was fixed in the first instance for the months from August to December 1995, and a 4% wage and salary rise was agreed from January 1996. In addition, the one-off payment (the so-called residual holiday bonus payment) was raised from 764 to 1600 from 1996, and a percentage rise in Christmas bonuses was brought forward to 1995. There were also special agreements reached for apprentices. Their pay was also increased by 4% for the second, third and fourth years from 1 January 1996, but there was no rise for the first year. In addition, there was a 1% increase in one-off payments and the Christmas bonus. The agreement on pay rises covers the period from 1 August 1995 to 31 July 1997.

Collective bargaining at Volkswagen

The 1995 round of collective bargaining at Volkswagen ended with a settlement after a five-week negotiating marathon. Overall, the negotiations were complex, difficult and extremely tough. There were times when there appeared to be little or no movement on either side from one negotiating session to the next. It was only in the final phase, during the final two negotiating rounds, that both sides began to move noticeably towards one another. There seemed to be a mutual understanding that the time to make decisions had arrived – either the negotiations would be concluded or they would have to be declared to have failed. There would have been no point in agreeing on any further extensions, as the positions of both sides on the issues concerned had been made clear at length and in detail. Thus it was ultimately this aggravated and tense situation which led to a settlement finally being reached. The gestation of the agreement and the variety and nature of its provisions bear the hallmark of the Volkswagen collective bargaining policy launched with the 1993 settlement and, indeed, constitute a further development of that approach.

Volkswagen's policy does not just pay lip-service to the concept of solidarity – it is a symbol of practical solidarity for the safeguarding and creation of jobs. Nothing is taboo provided it is acceptable – for the employer, the union and the workforce.

Thus Volkswagen's policy represents an approach focused on the employment market which is widely regarded by politicians, the media, employers and trade unions – and also by the public at large – as a crucially necessary development in industrial relations. In this context, the system of collective bargaining in Germany is often called into question – in particular the tradition of sectoral settlements – and there is talk of a crisis. Whilst it is correct to say that the system of collective agreements has, on the whole, proved itself and should not be abolished, some reform of the system of sectoral agreements is certainly required. But the solution is not to split up the system. Decentralisation of collective bargaining to plant level would alter the balance between employers and trade unions and would ulti-

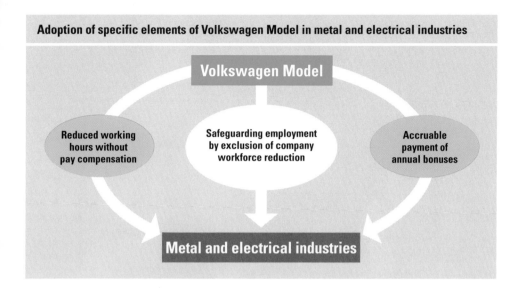

Adoption of specific elements of Volkswagen Model in metal and electrical industries

Volkswagen Model

Reduced working hours without pay compensation

Safeguarding employment by exclusion of company workforce reduction

Accruable payment of annual bonuses

Metal and electrical industries

mately contain more risks than opportunities. The solution can only lie in a new ranking of priorities and in the parties to the sectoral settlement opening up the scope of negotiations and allowing companies appropriate leeway to take the necessary action and make the necessary decisions.

The Volkswagen agreement demonstrates that a re-orientation of collective bargaining is possible. Developments at Volkswagen were, of course, made easier by the fact that the company negotiates and concludes its own collective agreements. This has been part of the Volkswagen tradition from the very outset and has often been severely criticised in the past. But it offers an opportunity to arrive at tailor-made solutions, and means that – unlike sectoral settlements – it is not necessary to take into account divergent company structures and interests. It is therefore possible to discuss and implement a re-orientation of policy more directly. For this reason as well as others, Volkswagen regards its tradition of company collective agreements as having been vindicated – despite the strong criticism levelled at it in the past.

The new life-curve

A new approach to lifetime employment and income

Traditional social security systems are becoming increasingly inappropriate, as variable forms of employment and new career structures develop. Now Volkswagen has come up with a new approach which enables an employee to draw on his lifetime's income and working time to provide cover for old age and the transition to retirement. A redrawing of the relationship between the individual and the company has resulted in a broad range of new possibilities – transfer of expertise, progressive work reduction programmes, variable or virtual models of employment, application of the acceptability curve, and participatory pension programmes.

The Volkswagen concept for the older employee

The ageing of the population in general – and the working population in particular – is a phenomenon observable in all countries of the European Union. The question of the role played by the older employees in a company – and in society – is going to become increasingly important. Patterns are changing so quickly that a rethink of the relationship between working and non-working life for older employees is called for. At present, society and social security systems still assume that full-time employment lasts for 35-45 years and involves steadily increasing income expectations – and that 63 or 65 could once again become the normal age of retirement.

The reality of the situation is rather different, and is proving a difficult challenge for social security systems throughout Europe. In western Germany, for example 25% of the unemployed, are elderly people. After the age of 45, people's career expectations already start to be oriented towards retirement. Age is a disadvantage to anyone seeking a job. The long-term unemployed look forward to the day when they will reach pensionable age. In the absence of any alternatives, early retirement is still one of the most widely accepted instruments for workforce downsizing. On the other hand, the fact that only 35% of people over the age of 60 are still in work indicates that it is not just the policies of major companies which are burdening the pension plans through their early retirement arrangements.

Instead of concentrating only on those with a long record of pension contributions, and imposing rigid age-limits or across-the-board late retirement programmes, scope should be created for giving the same treatment to those with variable-length careers as those who have spent their entire lives working.

Any new approach must involve a re-evaluation of the concept of lifetime salaries and lifelong working, and must ask the question: What do I need today – and what tomorrow? Diversity in careers is now no longer regarded as the exception to the rule: years taken up by education and military or social service, time spent caring for and bringing up children, phases of promotion, demotion and unemployment, periods spent in training, on sabbatical or on part-time work, time spent abroad or on assignment. So many periods of people's lives could be completely excluded from social security provisions or at least under-valued. New options need to be made available to the companies and employees concerned. Instead of the final age or last salary prior to retirement forming the basis for calculation of the pension, gradual transitions and variable combinations should be made possible. People's professional careers no longer necessarily peak just prior to retirement. There is scope for time and pension credits to be additionally accumulated from more active periods in an individual's career when his income was higher, or from inherited capital. The various stages of a person's life – youth, single adult, family, grown-up children, active old-age – can all be used to make reasonable provisions for old age and form part of the variable life-curve.

Despite the assumed decline in a person's career after the age of 45, human capital retains its value and can remain socially useful right up to and including involvement in virtual activities after the end of an individual's career. The Volkswagen model capitalises on the entire life-curve and provides for a new personnel policy suitable for the various generations within the workforce.

The following provisions are either planned or have been negotiated:

Volkswagen's Bauhof Centre provides scope for those who have completed their careers to involve themselves in social activities and virtual forms of employment within the ambit of the company.

- the prospect of employment for a predictable period of time for all employees under the Volkswagen Week system – instead of industry related reductions in the workforce
- the introduction of progressive phasing of careers for young and old to allow for longer utilisation of the experience and expertise of older colleagues
- the development of forms of work and training, and shift and block arrangements which are appropriate to the age of workers
- the linking of progressive work reduction programmes with new statutory regulations on phased early retirement
- the planning of the life-curve using the "work credit" programme, a degressive curve of reasonable income security and the opportunity to convert wages into pensions
- a cooperative and flexible approach to accruing providence capital through modular and participatory pension plans

- the creation of new types of relationship between older people and the company. Volkswagen has created a "round table" for this purpose, which brings together members of the public, trade unions, church representatives and institutions to look in particular at questions of creative leisure-time activities for the retired. This initiative is entitled EASI (engagiert, aktiv, sozial und interessiert = involved, active, socially minded and interested).

The demographic challenge

Forecasts confirm that the present aging process in the population will continue right into the middle of the next century. Despite immigration of foreign workers and an overall pattern of migration within Europe, the birth rate in Germany and the whole of Western Europe has stabilised at a very low level. Statistically speaking, to achieve even zero growth, each woman between the age of 15 and 45 would have to produce 2.1 children. But the present trend is towards 1.4 children in western Germany and 0.8 in the eastern part of the country. Thus a shrinking of the population is unavoidable. Every generation of parents is now larger than

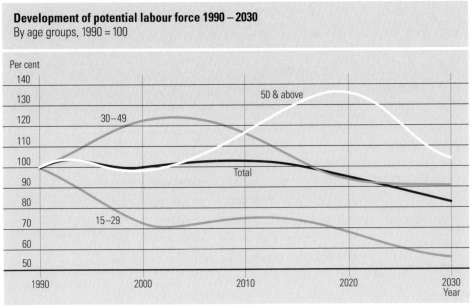

Development of potential labour force 1990 – 2030
By age groups, 1990 = 100

Per cent

Source: IAB 1995

that of their children. This means that the average age of the work-ing population will go up from the present 40 to about 50 by the year 2040, and the number of people over the age of 65 will rise rapidly from the present 20% to over 50%. These facts are com-mon knowledge – and so are the consequences. The contribution made by the younger generation to social security in order to care for the old is growing rapidly. Pension insurance contributions of 27% to 37% are forecast for the next 30 years, unless there is a drastic lowering of the level of statutory pensions. The "generation pact" is a two-way process. But one thing is certain: there is going to be a social security gap in the future, and no government, no union, no employer can afford to ignore this fact.

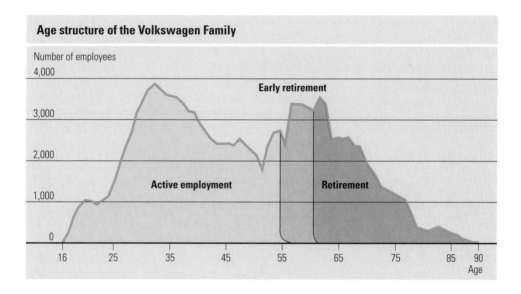

The corporate "extended family" is also beginning to feel the effects of this demographic shift. By the year 2010 there will be one company pensioner for every active employee still on the pay-roll. And when adjustments to pension contributions swallow up more money than a pay rise, the result could well be in conflict. But the positive side is even more significant – former employees will form the largest support group for the company. A fact that needs to be rediscovered.

Employment prospects for the elderly

The commercial success of the VW Beetle and the Golf has left Volkswagen with a legacy of 75,000 VW pensioners. It may be possible to delay its impact, but it is a development that can hardly be reversed before the year 2040. Even if the retirement age were extended to 63, the trend could not be stopped. All this would mean would be that the average age of the workforce would rise from the present 38 to 45 by the year 2005 and up to 18,000 more jobs would be required over the next ten years in Volkswagen AG's various plants. Older people would then find themselves competing with younger ones for scarce jobs. It is a problematic situation which could be solved by the Volkswagen Model.

These predicted developments mean that it is essential to develop some sort of plan for the elderly which allows them to stay in the company for longer but also provides for a gradual, phased exit from working life:

- training for older people
- use of the Personal Development Plan for securing expertise
- establishment of requirements and drafting of a plan for progressive work reduction

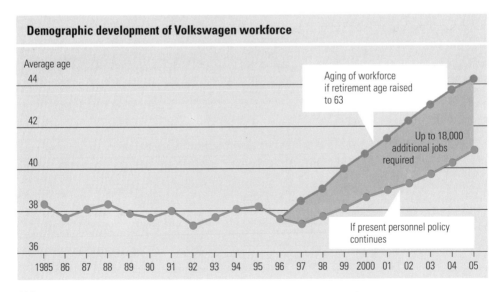

Demographic development of Volkswagen workforce

Average age

Aging of workforce if retirement age raised to 63

Up to 18,000 additional jobs required

If present personnel policy continues

- model projects and block programmes for personnel support and skills deployment
- health supervision, especially for shift workers

Then there is also a need to prepare for progressive early retirement. Here experience is being gathered with new forms of employment, as the original models for part-time working for older employees were poorly received by industry and workforces. An imaginative approach is required to find ways of introducing progressive work reduction for hundreds and thousands of people born in a particular year. This is nothing new to Volkswagen, as it has already had largely positive experiences with two years of progressive integration of apprentices after training. It can be done.

A lifetime's work and income – a new challenge

Without radical change, the principle of variable life-curves does not fit the present approach to provision for old-age. Loss of earnings as a result of the 4-day week, reduced income because of progressive work reduction prior to retirement, combined with other flexible elements in working arrangements, all mean that the basis for calculating later benefits is much reduced. Further-

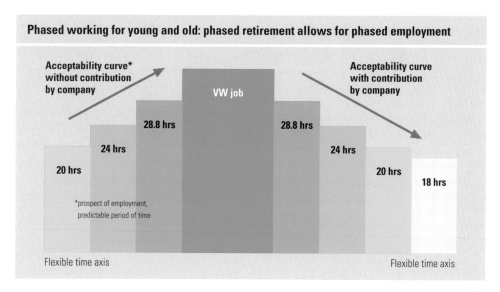

Phased working for young and old: phased retirement allows for phased employment

Acceptability curve* without contribution by company

VW job

Acceptability curve with contribution by company

28.8 hrs   28.8 hrs

24 hrs   24 hrs

20 hrs   20 hrs

18 hrs

*prospect of employment, predictable period of time

Flexible time axis   Flexible time axis

more, the length and nature of the transitional phase prior to statutory retirement need to be reconsidered. How should the reduced income of older employees in the period prior to retirement be compensated for? For how long can such bridging be provided in the form of additional payments, and what scope is there for contributions from other sources? The Volkswagen solution is as follows: every older member of the workforce can, for example, proceed to retirement after the age of 55 in three steps. These can take the form of 3 single years with 24-, 20- or 18-hour working weeks respectively. Or these phases can be taken as blocks. The route taken is established after consultation with the individual concerned and the works council. But the company must be able to apply such measures as are required, and retains control of their exact application. They can only be triggered if they are in the economic interests of the company or structural problems mean that the job is to be abolished.

For these progressive work reduction arrangements, additional payments according to the company's scale of acceptability apply. Irrespective of the total time involved, the employee receives a net compensation payment which ensures his income for the entire transitional phase prior to retirement. This approach is partly possible because the base for calculating this net compensation is the reduced income resulting from the 4-day week. The sums involved are thus significantly lower than former pension arrangements.

It is also possible to use "work credits" for these progressive work reduction arrangements. Additional work carried out by the employee during the previous five years is converted into "work credits" which can then be used for the phased retirement period. It is feasible for an individual to arrange to pass through the time-phases more rapidly, or to take retirement before he has reached the statutory age. These "work credits" constitute a sort of time-capital accumulated by older employees for early retirement.

For the first time this model offers an opportunity to use one's lifetime's work and income to solve the problems of transition into retirement. The financial provisions made for such claims are available at a later date – with payment triggered at the time of approval.

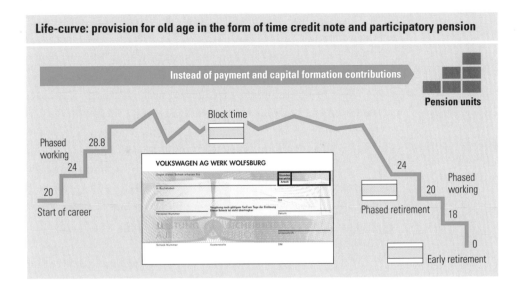

Life-curve: provision for old age in the form of time credit note and participatory pension

Instead of payment and capital formation contributions

Pension units

Block time

Phased working
28.8
24
20
Start of career

VOLKSWAGEN AG WERK WOLFSBURG

24
20
Phased retirement
Phased working
18
0
Early retirement

At Volkswagen the life-curve for the older employee would then be divided into the following phases: 50-55-60-65, with 50 marking the start of the "work credit" programme, 55 the beginning of the progressive work reduction plan, 60 early retirement, and 65 the definitive end of employment in the company.

The "building block" system

One of the biggest drawbacks of traditional systems of social benefits is their inflexibility.

In the past, Volkswagen has operated a so-called "final pay system" – a company pension was based on an individual's salary during the final twelve months prior to retirement. Under such a system the company only establishes what its commitment is going to be at the end of an individual's period of service. The result is that it has to constantly supplement its financing of the pension plan. It is estimated that a 10% to 15% under-financing of company pensions can easily occur. Given such uncertainty, the pension promised by the company is hardly ever increased, as the financial commitment involved has to be covered exclusively by pay developments in the distant future. In the past, the company had already reduced its final-pay commitment – by 40% for newly appointed staff from 1987 onwards. This reduction will take thirty years before it applies to the bulk of pensions and the effects are fully felt.

But it was obvious that such a system would fail completely if it had to be applied to variable patterns of working life and – above all – progressive work reduction arrangements. The final salary under such a phased programme would be far too low to be taken as a basis for calculating the pension, and would also not properly reflect the total work an individual had carried out during his entire period of service in the company. Action to remedy this situation was clearly required.Under the new, 1993 approach ("Every Job has a Face"), a "building block" scheme was presented as a possible solution. This has now been agreed on and came into force in January 1996.

The idea underlying this new company pension plan is that every year will be assessed separately and will form a single pension building block. The pension which an individual can later claim is then calculated on the basis of the annual return on this capital up to the time of retirement. This forms a reserve which assigns the expenditure fully to the year in question. Thus the financial outlay is a known quantity which can be planned for in advance, and there is no need for supplementary financing to cover past periods of service as a result of later salary rises or promotion.

An individual's entire working life can be represented by building blocks – some generated during good years for the company and others paid in by the employee himself. Nothing is lost – every year can be individually structured.

In accordance with an individual's salary growth, a series of pension blocks are produced over the years, which are available later to finance the pension.

As under this system the pension is based on an individual's entire working life and no pension blocks from the past are lost or – as happens in the "final pay" system – obliterated by later developments, it is admirably suited to the Volkswagen approach. An individual's entire working life can be reflected in pension blocks – derived from good years for the company, and from additional blocks purchased by the employee. Nothing is lost, and each year can be individually structured.

Thus it was possible to solve a central problem faced in the 1995 round of collective bargaining. Particular pension blocks can bridge the gap created by the phased transition to retirement. The block system fills the gap which phased retirement would otherwise have created. As in the case of other employees, blocks are created on the basis of the reduced wage resulting from the 28.8-hour week.

Another advantage of this new system is the simplicity and uniformity achieved by basing pensions on the curve of performance and income rather than on status groups.

Anyone with an above-average work record at Volkswagen during the course of his career can be sure of receiving an above-average pension, irrespective of whether he opts for progressive work reduction. And the same parameters apply to the entire workforce – management and workers alike: the same table of pension payments, the same actuarial calculations, the same range of benefits – the only differentiation being in the year's income taken as the basis for calculation of the pension. This also takes into account the fact that a considerable part of the annual income of managers consists of bonus-related pay and is not reflected in the monthly salary which forms the basis for assessment of the pension.

The old regulations have been incorporated into the new system and form a wage-related base block. All employees under the age of 55 can switch to the new system. As a general rule, the longer one is in the new system, the better off one is in comparison.

Participatory pension plan

The new system is tailor-made for the addition of extra blocks paid for by the employee. The participatory pension plan offers this option. In the Volkswagen Model this brings identical benefits and the same level of insurance as the unit system. It is the first system of social benefits designed for a new lifetime employment curve.

The heavy burden of taxation and other levies on personal income means that personal pension schemes paid for from disposable net income do not achieve the level of benefits that would be necessary to fill the gap.

The basic principle involved in a participatory pension is that a person's claim to payment or social benefits today is replaced by a pension unit for tomorrow. This must apply to benefits not yet received or pension rights which the individual cannot control like savings, but which are set aside for cases of death, invalidity and retirement. This further element of provision can be built up out of untaxed income, and thus has a higher yield than any other form of investment.

The participatory pension can be built up from negotiated salary or additional allowances such as capital formation contributions. The Volkswagen Model managed to provide a bridge to a new kind of pension programme by dissolving the existing agreement on capital formation contributions – and the prospects that this will become a permanent arrangement are good.

By sacrificing DM 32 net per month (DM 52 gross capital formation), an additional company pension of DM 140 to DM 625 can be acquired. A 25-year-old receives a higher figure than a 45-year-old, on account of the longer period involved.

This participatory pension could also develop advantageously via collective bargaining, as the unusually high leverage it possesses means that consensus is easier to reach than on other sub-

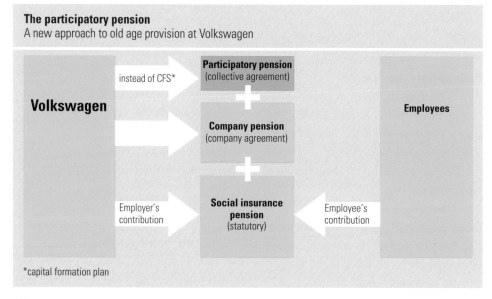

The participatory pension
A new approach to old age provision at Volkswagen

Volkswagen

instead of CFS*

Participatory pension
(collective agreement)

Company pension
(company agreement)

Employer's contribution

Social insurance pension
(statutory)

Employee's contribution

Employees

*capital formation plan

jects. In the past, the entire Volkswagen company pension programme with a total of DM 5 billion accrued rights could have been built up from a wage increase of 3% to 4%, whereas the new programme creates 1.5% to 1.6% for the employee for each percentage point of wage increase. No other instrument is as effective as this combination of pre-tax financing and returns at the long-term capital-market interest rate of 7.5%.

Volkswagen participatory pension compared with other forms of provision

Volkswagen participatory plan	161 %
Direct insurance	131 %
Capital formation plan	100 %
Bank savings account	100 %
Social security pension	65 %

100 %

result in benefits

Value of contributions	100 %

Basis: Annual income of DM 60,000

Basis for calculation of social security pension:
- insurance starts at age of 20
- retirement age 65
- contribution indexed at 3%
- interest on contributions 7% p.a.

Source: calculations by Dr. Bode / Dr. Grabner & Partner

In the medium term, the unit and participatory pension plans also mean that the company builds up extra capital – and at the same time costs remain stable, as subsequent revaluation of pension rights already acquired is not possible.

Uniquely for Germany, Volkswagen has found an opening in the collective bargaining arena for this innovative concept of securing the future.

In view of the storm-clouds gathering over the state pension plan, one question is becoming increasingly urgent: How can those concerned still actively exert an influence on the level of pension they will eventually receive?

The two plans just described offer scope for deliberately balancing present and future income.

New relationship between work and leisure

Under the system of flexible life-time working, the balance between work and leisure time is constantly shifting. The Volkswagen Week involves on average 28.8 of the 168 hours available to individuals each week. As a person grows older, there is also a redistribution of work over the year, with a heavier workload in the spring and possibly even during normal holiday periods, but this is balanced by many weeks of time off. The time available for new activities outside the place of work expands enormously. But older employees still tend to maintain the bonds linking them to colleagues, neighbours and family right up to the end of their working lives. Anyone who has dedicated decades of his life to working for a common objective will find it difficult to break these last ties. This close identification with the section of Volkswagen in which one worked creates a strong sympathy for the company in the towns where its plants are located. And it is a feeling which runs right through every club and car-sharing programme. Life inside the company overlaps with life outside. It is important to recognise this and capitalise on it for the period of preparation for retirement and for actual retirement itself.

A new perspective on aging – the Bauhof Centre

Retirement inevitably involves a process of reorientation. To help support this process, Volkswagen launched the EASI initiative – which aims to open up a dialogue about new perspectives for active old people. Volkswagen alone has some 25,000 ex-employees, who still have more than 20 years of active life ahead of them. In Wolfsburg, for example, some 36% of the population is now over the age of 50. The aim of this dialogue and discussion is to rediscover the productive capacity of old age and channel this into social projects. It also offers an opportunity for those concerned to work together and discover the joys of self-organisation outside the context of the daily grind. The Bauhof Centre which has been set up is intended to become a meeting point, an information and advice centre, and a source of projects and ideas on health. This pioneering project was launched in 1996 by Volkswagen, BKK (the VW health insurance company) and the City of Wolfsburg.

BAUHOF
Centre
for Active
Health Promotion

The future of old-age provision

Demographic developments, increased life-expectancy and the trend towards variable working lives require changes to the system of old age provision. The doubling of the proportion of old people in the population over the coming decades will necessitate either a doubling of pension contributions or a halving of benefits. Furthermore, the system of old-age provision also has to cope with the consequences of German reunification and the integration of immigrants. And these additional burdens on the system are not matched by any additional contributions. There is also an additional problem of an increasing rate of retirement due to health reasons or unemployment. Above all, it has been the trend towards early retirement which has triggered a rethink. In the past, the response has been for the government to introduce new legislation or the courts to pass judgements placing restrictions on early retirement or making it more expensive.

Faced with this situation, Volkswagen has developed its own proposals on how a balance could be achieved between the interests of the various parties involved. Unless this question is resolved, there is a danger of millions joining the ranks of the unemployed, as even in eastern Germany early retirement has been used as a – legally sanctioned – form of employment policy.

If every person at present taking early retirement were to work right up to the flexible age of retirement, this would tie up jobs for a further five to eight years and have a devastating effect on unemployment. Moreover, an increase in youth unemployment has a far greater potential for causing social unrest than a sensitively managed system of early retirement. This consideration – which forms the basis of the Volkswagen approach – leads to a search for potential solutions which are acceptable to all concerned but at the same time constitute an alternative to the present system of early retirement. Clearly, the overall effect should be to reduce the burden on the social security system.

Continued high unemployment rates and slow growth in the creation of new jobs mean that there is little point in legislating against early retirement. This would merely mean that instead of several hundred thousand "early" pensioners, the labour market would be flooded with an additional number of young unemployed people.

This was the background against which Volkswagen put forwards its proposals for old-age provision in the spring of 1995. It is a programme which aims at linking the scope for older employees to be phased out of work on a variable basis with the securing of jobs for younger people. The underlying idea is that if all those concerned can make a contribution, there need be no major disadvantages for anyone. For politicians and the social security system it means that the financial burden is reduced while at the same time an acceptable solution for the other parties is forthcoming. The employees' contribution consists of a reasonable loss of income during the transition to retirement, plus a willingness to put some of their own money towards the additional funding required. This gives them a prospect of a dignified transition to retirement without going through any period of unemployment. It also allows for the older generation to hand on jobs for their children and grandchildren. Movement between the generations on the labour market would not grind to a halt.

From the point of view of the companies it must be more acceptable to contribute towards maintaining early retirement as a method of adjustment and renewal of the workforce than to have to take measures to cut down on the number of young workers – with all the concomitant potential for social conflict. The phased working programme is made up of the following elements:

The state would have to make it possible to claim partial pension rights at an earlier age and to receive a full pension at the age of 60 – and indeed provisions for this are contained in the proposed amendments to the relevant law. The additional financial burden resulting from this flexibilisation of old age provision through a progressive system of early retirement would have to be recouped, partly through acceptable levels of actuarial deductions from the pension – provided these were confined to the additional burden only. And at the same time, incentives would need to be created for all those cases involving refilling of jobs or securing of employment. In this case, continued payments of tax and other contributions ensure that the model operates economically. Here companies would need to be granted greater scope to cover some of the costs from tax relief, for example in the form of tax exemptions related to the taking on of apprentices after training or appropriate promotion of part-time employment (labour promotion contracts). And employees could also make a

The proposal involves the introduction of a phased approach to work which benefits both young and old. Based on Volkswagen's experience, this model requires a contribution from politicians, companies and employees. The benefits are an improved labour market situation and a lightening of the load borne by the social security system.

Phased working for young and old

- Attractive model for all involved
- Effective safeguarding of jobs
- Lightens load on labour administration and state budget

Government	Company	Employee
• Tax relief or support under labour promotion law for part-time work above age of 55	• Participation requirement: commitment to take on apprentices or unemployed	• Flexibility and acceptable contribution
• Flexibilisation of retirement age/removal of requirement to have been previously unemployed for social security pension to be payable after age of 60	• Payment of additional allowance on top of salary	• Solidarity with younger generation
• Earlier entitlement to reduced pension from age of 58	• Willingness to top up contributions or adopt joint approach to old-age provision	• Part-financing of model, e.g. via participatory pension

Model of phased working programme for young and old

contribution via the acceptability curve, accumulated time credits and the participatory pension plan – as in the case of Volkswagen. However, this requires unions and management to take the initiative and the state to facilitate the process by clarifying the situation in the laws on company pensions and the labour promotion law (i.e. no consideration of time saved during short time working).

Calculations confirm that all these various elements could combine to create a new, acceptable compromise. Such a solution would be more helpful than a law which did not enjoy a broad degree of acceptance and ran the risk of failure. In view of the enormous problems Germany faces in retaining its attractiveness as a manufacturing location, it would be well worth finding an effective compromise such as formed the basis of the 1992 pension reform.

The Volkswagen World

A corporate manifesto for everyone

"We in the Volkswagen World, with our 5 brands, dedicate ourselves to developing, manufacturing and marketing the world's best quality and most attractive vehicles, at reasonable prices. We aim to achieve the greatest possible success in global markets with our available resources. The people of the Volkswagen World are striving to secure stable and stimulating working, learning and living conditions for long-term. We want our children and grandchildren to inherit an environmentally-safe planet. This is our commitment."

A common commitment

The Volkswagen World embraces a total of 240,000 people in 296 companies – all of them individuals who are dedicated to their work, and have their own personal expectations and family responsibilities. This is the company's human capital. And it is important that they should be able to identify with their work and their company. To this end, Volkswagen has formulated a manifesto which applies throughout the Volkswagen World and is comprehensible in all languages. It constitutes a commitment covering all brands and regions. Top management throughout the Group has committed itself to the ideas contained in this summary of everything that the Volkswagen culture stands for. It is a crystallisation of what this global company believes in.

Our Volkswagen World

"We in the Volkswagen World, with our 5 brands, dedicate ourselves to developing, manufacturing and marketing the world's best quality and most attractive vehicles, at reasonable prices. We aim to achieve the greatest possible success in global markets with our available resources. The people of the Volkswagen World are striving to secure stable and stimulating working, learning and living conditions for long-term. We want our children and grandchildren to inherit an environmentally-safe planet.

This is our commitment."

The manifesto was developed at the Group Top Management Conference in 1994, and, following discussions at local level, was confirmed a year later.

Everywhere – in Asia-Pacific, North and South America, Africa and Europe – for all five brands: Volkswagen, Audi, SEAT, Skoda and Commercial Vehicles – the driving force for the company is its markets and its people. Its aim is to achieve maximum market success and offer a secure home to its employees. And it attaches high priority to treating the environment with care, so that it can hand on to future generations a world which they can live in. These are the guiding principles for everything the company and its workforce does. They underline Volkswagen's role as the world's fourth largest vehicle manufacturer and as a global player.

It summarises the essence of the company's ambitious vision for the future. It contains all the essential elements, and can be translated into all languages and cultures. Its fascination stems from the fact that it is accessible and comprehensible to everyone.

This corporate manifesto reflects the way Volkswagen views its role in the world – but it does more than just that: it also determines Volkswagen's attitude within the company and the expectations made of the various brands and regions, the 296 companies in the Group, and top management. Here, too, the manifesto spells out the commitment of the owners of the company to providing leadership and achieving the goals it has set. Of course, the Supervisory and Executive Boards of Volkswagen AG also bear responsibility vis-à-vis their shareholders for running the company. Control of affiliated companies is one of the basic obligations of ownership. But precisely how the entire complex of companies is run is one of the crucial elements of corporate culture. And here guidelines are called for:

- We aim to use our skills to realise the goals of the company. For everyone in the Volkswagen Family – whatever the brand, region, subsidiary or plant – this means operating according to the principle of "Everyone is as free as his degree of competence allows". In other words: an individual's skill and competence can and must define that person's freedom to act. If problems begin to multiply, the company can then offer increasing support – eventually taking over direct responsibility if necessary.
- We aim to realise the goals of the company on the basis of consensus: "Everyone is guided by the agreed minimum standards". The precise nature of these minimum standards has been defined for key areas – including personnel issues. When must I inform others, when must I consult others, when do I need the company's approval or agreement? These are rules of

Volkswagen's corporate manifesto guidelines

Volkswagen World

Competence

"Everyone is as free as his degree of competence allows"

Consensus

"Everyone is guided by the agreed minimum standards"

Cooperation

"Everyone supports a networked cooperation"

Proprietary rights and sole responsibility: Volkswagen AG

the game which everyone must take to heart if they are to contribute to achieving consensus.

- We aim to realise the goals of the company on the basis of cooperation: "Everyone supports a networked cooperation". The setting of strategic objectives and the process of corporate planning are collaborative tasks which need to enjoy the support of all concerned. Thus, an internal process of networking draws all elements of the Volkswagen World closer together. In addition to Specialist Steering groups, the Group Top Management Conference and the Group Executive Forum are the two bodies within which top managers cooperate over setting objectives for the company and maintaining the impetus of the transformation process.

The VW commitment – often personally signed – is visible proof of a determination to realise the common objectives developed by the company.

The basic rules laid down in the manifesto provide clear guidelines for cooperation within the company. The system is controllable, and guarantees a certain stability of trust. But it relies on those involved knowing each other. Trust also thrives on shared familiarity with the demands made by business in global markets – and these are based on success at local level.

Transformation process
From functional organisation to value-added processes

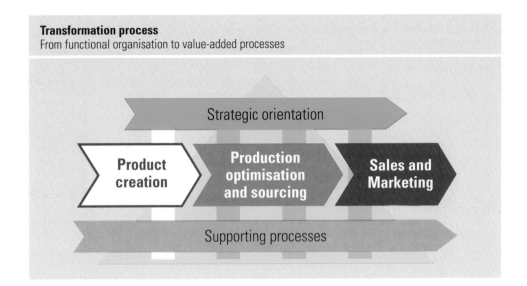

Strategic orientation

Product creation

Production optimisation and sourcing

Sales and Marketing

Supporting processes

Globalisation of the company – internationalisation of management

A successful globalisation strategy must begin at home. It has to build on a realisation that you rely on other people in the world. You have to think internationally, to be willing to share responsibility for the company's further development on a global scale. A senior manager's workplace is the entire Volkswagen World. And every employee's job depends on the Volkswagen World too – on its image, its products, its investments, its suppliers, its sales networks, its quality assurance and expertise.

Thinking in international dimensions is what keeps the whole thing going. Where can one find the best employees to help expand the company? Who needs to get to know the Group and operations at one of its locations better in order to get on in his career? Who needs training – when his international focus is Germany?

Internationalisation requires individuals to be interested in the world beyond the confines of Volkswagen, to want to get to know about markets, competitors and the entire operating environment. We must have 10% to 20% of Volkswagen's best brains available for collaborative ventures and new projects and processes. But will this be enough to make the necessary human capital available for the Group's future?

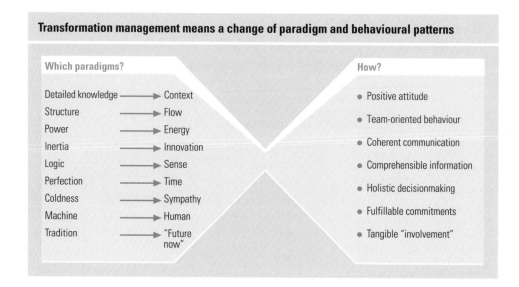

Transformation management means a change of paradigm and behavioural patterns

Which paradigms?		How?
Detailed knowledge ⟶ Context		• Positive attitude
Structure ⟶ Flow		• Team-oriented behaviour
Power ⟶ Energy		• Coherent communication
Inertia ⟶ Innovation		• Comprehensible information
Logic ⟶ Sense		• Holistic decisionmaking
Perfection ⟶ Time		• Fulfillable commitments
Coldness ⟶ Sympathy		• Tangible "involvement"
Machine ⟶ Human		
Tradition ⟶ "Future now"		

It is important that Volkswagen should systematically create and promote an international management network. The company has long since started organising development programmes for international managers. In the past, the main focus was on internationalising German managers, and 27% of VW managers have now gained experience abroad, with 20% management replacement candidates undergoing international training. And the number is growing all the time. But this one-way process will soon end. Plans are in hand to ensure that there is also a flow in the opposite direction. By setting targets for each company, it is intended to achieve a greater degree of internationalisation throughout the Group.

Globalisation must go beyond just an inner circle. Internationalisation is not an end in itself. A "company that breathes" commits itself to responding to the needs of its customers worldwide.

To support this process, an International Trainee and Personnel Development Programme has been set up. During the first 18 months at Volkswagen, every graduate trainee has to work on a project abroad. Management replacement candidate programmes also require mobility and involve job rotation abroad. And every year, specialist and management personnel is recruited for international assignments via international job advertisements. The main countries for such assignments are, in order of frequency:

the Czech Republic, Mexico, Spain, China, Portugal and Brazil. According to US surveys, about 40% of postings abroad fail because the selection process was inadequate – or even non-existent. For this reason, a system of selection for postings abroad based on the VW Assessment Centre for management has now been developed – with the aim of reducing the failure quota and enhancing the status of such postings.

The system also aims to increase the degree to which those posted abroad are accepted by their host companies – and also to facilitate subsequent reintegration when they return. The success of the individual concerned in attaining this – or in continuing up the international career ladder – is a crucial aspect of the credibility of this internationalisation process. Mobility must not be perceived to be a punishment or a handicap for somebody's career. For these expatriates, the Personal Development Plan plays an important role – allowing later opportunities or offers to be recorded.

The internationalisation of German companies still frequently comes up against the limitations imposed by German national law. It should involve taking on full responsibility wherever one is required within the Volkswagen World, but before a German com

Developing international management

Management development international networks
- Group Junior Executive Programme
- Group Executive Forum
- Group Top Management Conference

Development of High Potentials
- International Trainee Programme
- High-Potential Programme
- International Personnel Development Programme
- Young People Team

Development of international management

Example programmes
- Technology Transfer Agreement
- Volkswagen International Training and Development Programme, South Africa

Know-how transfer and development
- International deployment of personnel
- Foreign Service Employees
- Assignments

pany can put together its international development team, it first has to establish – in the case of non-European managers – that there is nobody available on the German market with comparable qualifications. Before a Mexican logistics expert can swap jobs with a German colleague so as to ensure that CKD parts supply runs more smoothly, he first has to challenge many legislative obstacles. Not all countries have yet relaxed their legislation to allow for globalisation of management. It is almost easier to send work around the world via the information highway than to organise a genuinely international team for a particular geographical location.

An important contribution to internationalisation of the Volkswagen World is made by Group Management Development. The Group Junior Executive Programme enables young managers who display a high degree of potential for international work to spend nine months working together on seminar modules and projects on topics of relevance to the future of the company. The sponsor – and at the same time the customer – for each project is a top manager. Performance assessments result in the very best being taken into the talent pool for key positions within the Group. And then there are the projects developed and launched

International personnel deployment
A measure for developing international management

Home company

Manpower planning
• Personal Development Plan

Reintegration
• timely planning
• better selection
• commitment by divisions

Personnel selection
following multiple
assessment principle

**Preparation for
assignment abroad**
• intercultural,
language, medical
• "look & see" trip

Host company
ongoing assistance – also
by personnel department
of home company

+ Benchmarking – optimisation of contracts and remuneration

The Personal Development Plan enables agreements on elements of mobility

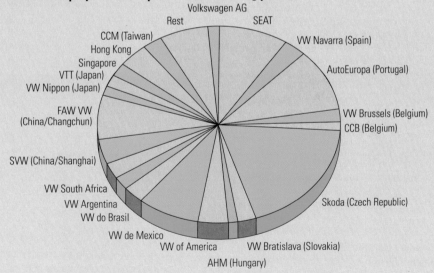

Elements of mobility

International job locations

	Worldwide	Europe	North-America	S.-America/Africa	Asia-Pacific
Up to now:	□	□	□	□	□
Personal wish/readiness:	□ □	□ □	□ □	□ □	□ □

National job locations

Up to now:

Personal wish:

Job rotation

planned (PL) possible (PO)	1995	1996	1997	1998	1999	2000	2001	2002	2003	2004

Languages

0: Native Speaker
1: Negotiating Level
2: Intermediate Level
3: Basic Knowledge

International deployments take place in the following places:

Volkswagen AG
Rest
SEAT
CCM (Taiwan)
Hong Kong
Singapore
VTT (Japan)
VW Nippon (Japan)
FAW VW (China/Changchun)
SVW (China/Shanghai)
VW South Africa
VW Argentina
VW do Brasil
VW de Mexico
VW of America
AHM (Hungary)
VW Bratislava (Slovakia)
Skoda (Czech Republic)
CCB (Belgium)
VW Brussels (Belgium)
AutoEuropa (Portugal)
VW Navarra (Spain)

by Senior Executive Forums. By holding such forums several times per year and restricting participation to a small number of managers, it is possible to offer high-quality, top-level group coaching.

For those in the Volkswagen World there is no such thing as a foreign country. Distances are irrelevant. A customer in the US is just as important as one in Lower Saxony. It is a world which continues to shrink – every manager and every location can be reached within seconds or at the most 24-hours, thanks to tele-mail, video-conferencing, and modern air travel.

A qualitatively new form of mutual help and learning is developing within the Volkswagen Group. All the personnel managers know each other all over the world, meet regularly and work in close collaboration with one another within a worldwide network which defines the responsibilities and links between them. Six "Centres of Competence" provide specialist support for this worldwide system of personnel management and assume complete or partial responsibility for central tasks requiring coordination. All personnel managers support the principle of mutual

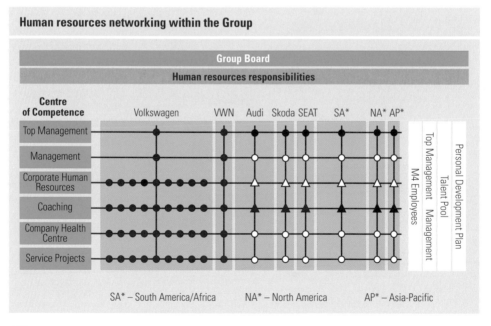

Human resources networking within the Group

SA* – South America/Africa   NA* – North America   AP* – Asia-Pacific learning and share a belief in the importance of improving personnel procedures, expanding the pool of talent and upgrading the quality of the workforce.

Employee participation on an international scale

It is not just the personnel management which cooperates on a personal basis worldwide – workforce representatives also operate globally, with the total support of the management. World Conferences, European Works Council meetings and sessions of plant works councils have for many years now ensured the participation of the workforce throughout the operations of the entire Group.

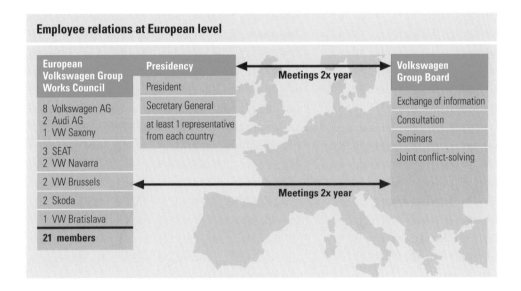

Employee relations at European level

European Volkswagen Group Works Council	Presidency		Volkswagen Group Board
	President	Meetings 2x year	
8 Volkswagen AG	Secretary General		Exchange of information
2 Audi AG	at least 1 representative from each country		Consultation
1 VW Saxony			Seminars
3 SEAT			Joint conflict-solving
2 VW Navarra			
2 VW Brussels			
2 Skoda		Meetings 2x year	
1 VW Bratislava			
21 members			

Within Volkswagen there is also a Volkswagen World for employees. Union membership runs at some 80% of the Volkswagen workforce worldwide. Since 1976 Volkswagen AG has encouraged international cooperation amongst works councils, and in 1992 this led to the setting up of a European Works Council for the Group, which now covers all Volkswagen's European manufacturing operations. The emphasis here is on dialogue and a flow of information about corporate planning processes and new approaches to personnel issues. On several occasions seminars have been organised to examine specific aspects of corporate strategy in greater depth. In the preamble to the agreement signed by the Group Board and the European Works Council it is stated that competitiveness has to be achieved via high productivity and flexibility, combined with increased standards of product quality and environmental compatibility. This is also seen as forming the basis for successful social development and the company's ability to meet its obligations vis-à-vis the workforce.

In addition to involving international employee representatives in forward planning processes and the formulation of corporate strategy, the aim was to achieve general acceptance that everyone shares responsibility for retaining competitiveness. In all plants, works councils need to lend their full support to new instruments such as CIP^2, global sourcing and business plans for reducing costs and improving quality. The European Works Council constitutes a forum in which all new personnel decisions for the various plants can be discussed constructively. CIP^2 has now been introduced everywhere, often on the basis of similar agreements. Global sourcing and forward sourcing have now also been accepted. Usually a "last call" based on the German plant agreement is made, which gives a plant faced with job cuts a last chance to draw up a package of measures in collaboration with the works council, aimed at expanding production volume by improving the plant's competitive position.

Symposia focusing on operations in particular locations are now held throughout the Group, with the aim of involving the local workforce representatives more deeply in introducing process improvements. European Works Councils share responsibility for the success of the company and the survival of particular plants – undoubtedly an unusual change of roles for some countries.

At least once a year, symposia or similar meetings are organised between the works council and the management, which offer an opportunity to discuss strategy and measures to protect operations in a particular location and draw up a plan for solving problems over the year to come. Such developments have long since demonstrated that the Volkswagen World is not just there for the managers – it represents an invitation to everyone to become involved in shaping the future of the company. The M4 model applies everywhere: creativity means enabling the workforce to participate increasingly in company affairs; multi-skilled also means facilitating the acquisition of experience and the transfer of knowledge throughout the Group – and this includes the works councils; Mobility knows no bounds. If the works council in a distant country is able to achieve a skilful resolution of difficult labour conflicts, then this is given full support by the company. A feeling that people of different nationalities and culture are respected within a company and are able to work together as a team is something which has far-reaching effects beyond the shop floor. Volkswagen is concerned to establish a good reputation in this respect too.

The future

Every job has a customer. No customer – no job. How can we win new customers? This is the crucial question which needs to be asked in the context of saving jobs. The concept of the "company that breathes" is a response to the problem. It is an approach which centres on the customer and views success as depending crucially on a change of attitude and an orientation of a company's entire range of products, processes and developments towards the customer. What distinguishes a successful company from its competitors is that it is better, faster, more cost-effective and more innovative. It is responsive to markets and customers' wishes – in a nutshell: it is up-to-date.

The route to new jobs is via the customer. It is the customer who ultimately decides whether a particular manufacturing location is going to survive. We want the customer to come back to us – rather than the product. We want to find ways of attracting even more customers. We have to learn to breathe with the customer, to feel the pulse of the marketplace in every job. The work of every single employee has to withstand scrutiny by the customer. It is not enough simply to be customer-oriented – not enough to be moving in the right direction – we have to actually deliver the goods – literally and metaphorically. And we must realise that the nature of our customers has changed radically. We now operate in a buyer's market, and the result has been a price revolution. Any room to manoeuvre as far as our costings are concerned now has to benefit the customer – not us. And the customer has also caused tremendous upheavals in the field of quality. Products which were tolerated yesterday are rejected today. Customers have developed a new self-confidence. You can have problems with your staff, problems with anyone – but not with the customer. It costs more to win back a lost customer than to satisfy him in the first place. Customers expect products to retain their value. Every purchase is an investment in the future, and loses value more slowly if it comes from a successful company. Product image, re-sale value, warranties are valued more highly – and can attract a higher price.

There are many things you can do to improve a particular lo-cation and raise levels of employment – but you will only succeed if you manage to please the customer. He is the invisible third party who is present at all discussions about the "alliance for jobs", all wage negotiations and works agreements. And he is not there merely as an observer. So it is better to talk about him, and consider what you can do to be more responsive to his needs.

A breathing company offers scope for considering what can reasonably be expected of the workforce and what is feasible for the company as a whole, in terms of offering more to the cus-tomer. Greater flexibility with regard to working hours, higher productivity, better quality, reduced costs rather than scaled-down workforces. Otherwise the customer will not be willing to part with his money. It is the reverse of the usual purchasing-power formula – the customer is no longer prepared to make any con-cessions, so he has to be attracted by greater value-added. What counts is quality produced by team work. A critical employee also makes a critical customer – all we want to do is merge these two roles once again. If the product manufactured by an employee is to withstand scrutiny by him as a customer, then he has to put as much work into manufacturing it as he would expect from an-other company whose customer he might be.

It is possible to bring both interests into line with each other – market success and success as an employee. If you want the one, you must be prepared to talk about the other. Win-win situa-tions are possible, if other values are considered in addition to pay. For example the value of a secure job, or the value of a cus-tomer – which is necessary for the creation of new jobs.

There is wide scope here for agreement between employers and employees who are determined to serve the customer – without having to suffer for it. Quality, service, variability – and many other concepts – are relevant here.

Surveys have revealed that we urgently need to rethink many of the roles we play. Employees often regard collective bargaining and discussions with employers as a kind of ritual from which they do not expect very much personal benefit and which they tend to view with a degree of scepticism.

There is a lack of conviction that the real problems are being tackled. And indeed you are doomed to failure if, as happened in the past, the customer is excluded from the calculation, or an attempt is even made to reach agreement at his expense. Those days are now over. Responsibility has to be taken for compromises – it cannot simply be passed on to others. But we should regard all this as a positive development. The customer must be involved. A breathing company adopts a different approach to wage policy and focuses on all those aspects which offer scope for employers and employees to pull together in the same direction.

The new areas of consensus are what hold the two partners in industry together. The pressure to reach agreement is irresistible. More group work, greater participation in corporate pro-

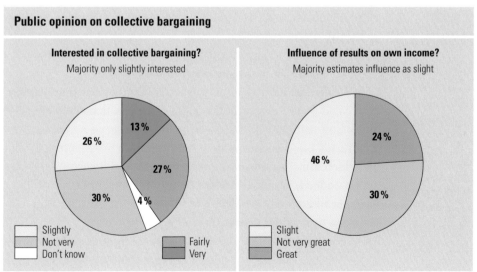

Public opinion on collective bargaining

Interested in collective bargaining?
Majority only slightly interested

13 %
26 %
27 %
30 %
4 %

Slightly
Not very
Don't know
Fairly
Very

Influence of results on own income?
Majority estimates influence as slight

24 %
46 %
30 %

Slight
Not very great
Great

Source: FORSA, 1995

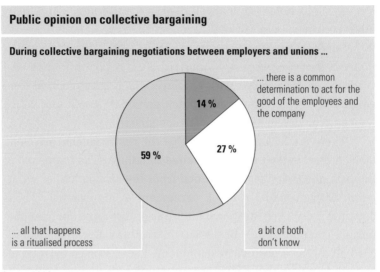

Public opinion on collective bargaining

During collective bargaining negotiations between employers and unions ...

... there is a common determination to act for the good of the employees and the company

14 %

27 %

59 %

... all that happens is a ritualised process

a bit of both don't know

Source: FORSA, 1995

cesses, collaboration over cost-savings – all these are steps towards a redefinition of work processes and introduction of greater autonomy into them. Gone are the days when such an approach was rejected – or greeted with a superior smile. It has now been fully accepted by all concerned. And it reflects the shift from rigid hierarchical structures to ones based on competence. Companies have now become so transparent that nobody can hide behind his authority any longer. Commands are replaced by commitment. Entrepreneurial dynamism is more important than ordered procedures which tie up unnecessary capacity.

If the customer now plays such a central role, then companies need to be released from rigid contracts and obligations. A breathing company is supposed to be capable of adapting. And this raises the question of how really competitive a company can be which aims at preserving employment and operating a 4-day week. Indeed, to what extent can any responsible entrepreneur promise to maintain employment? Does the Volkswagen Model inhibit the innovation process?

The last thing the Volkswagen Model intends to be is inflexible. On the contrary, it aims to create time for creativity on a hitherto unknown scale. Greater control over time is accompanied, for the particularly creative fields of development, by a high degree of autonomy. But deployment of human resources nevertheless has to be subject to discipline, careful costing and strict budgeting, if productivity is to be maintained.

The criteria for preserving jobs in a breathing company are extremely diverse: For Volkswagen, the important ones were:

- The Volkswagen tradition – i.e. the particular atmosphere of trust relating to employees and their representatives is a valuable asset – for the future too.
- If it comes to dismissals, labour law protects not the top expertise and the best performers but rather the socially weakest in a company. Indeed the employees who are most important to a company are likely to be lost.
- Power relations are always an important factor in stability: when the going gets tough, the management and crew need to calmly go about their duty without getting over-excited.
- The aim is to cut costs not jobs – i.e. the workforce representatives help reduce costs but in doing so help preserve jobs.
- Preservation of jobs is guaranteed for a predictable and plannable period of two years. This is a sensible way of reducing the risk. It is still possible to negotiate, but using other, socially acceptable measures, rather than the usual ones.
- The company retains its full scope for taking action. At any time it can go beyond the 4-day week and breathe more deeply. But it can also move in the opposite direction, by expanding the other elements in the collective agreement (early retirement, progressive retirement, short time working, work credits).
- Both entrepreneurs and trade unions have to think long and hard about how to preserve jobs. Faced with millions of unemployed, both sides clearly have a considerable moral obligation to take action. The most ethical solution is for both to look beyond questions of wage costs and working hours and find areas of agreement which free up creativity and dynamism.
- To preserve jobs via variability and acceptability also means flexibility to take up alternative jobs within and outside the company. The mobility to go where the jobs are is part and parcel of this approach.

A breathing company makes a virtue out of a necessity. Employment and working hours have been defined and accepted at a low level of 28.8 hours, but at any time it is possible to take a deeper breath. The Volkswagen Week is intended to stabilise the initial compromise at an economically and socially acceptable level.

Under this approach, personnel managers and works council members become team leaders. And the breathing company will have several entrepreneurial roles to offer in the future: time planner, service provider, coaching developer, manpower assignment planner. No human capital can afford to be wasted when the company starts to breathe. And the people playing these roles will work in free collaboration with the local management. What is needed is the courage to make full use of the personnel and M4 resources available. Every manager thus becomes a personnel manager – responsible for running a virtual workforce. From work organisation to time-planning, he has to solve personnel matters directly with those concerned – in conjunction with the works council. Overall entrepreneurial responsibility and the involvement of the workforce are perfectly compatible nowadays.

Since 1993 the Volkswagen approach has survived its toughest test. Implementation of the original personnel plan has been virtually completed. Now new ideas and agreements are being drawn up with equal energy. "Every Job has a Face" – that was a plea for social responsibility at a time of crisis. Now a new motto – "Every Job has a Customer" – provides the basis for a long-term strategy aimed at achieving the sort of success vis-à-vis the customer which brings the prospect of greater job security.

Table of contents

As an aid to understanding the model collective agreement for the "company that breathes", we have reproduced here the most important agreements signed between Volkswagen AG and the metalworkers' union IG Metall.

Following the collective negotiations between Volkswagen AG and IG Metall in 1995, the following settlement was reached on 12th September 1995. It contains amongst other things agreements on the following topics: continuation of the 28.8-hour week, employment safeguards, introduction of the Volkswagen Week, increases in wages and salaries, and other important core elements covered by the collective bargaining (e.g. time credit notes, performance contribution by employees, phased integration of apprentices into full employment, phased working programme for older employees, working time principles, remuneration principles).

This settlement was used as the basis for implementation in the form of new collective contracts and agreements.

Major collective agreements resulting from the 1995 settlement

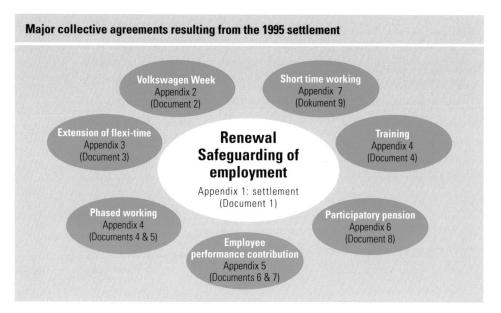

Volkswagen Week
Appendix 2
(Document 2)

Short time working
Appendix 7
(Dokument 9)

Extension of flexi-time
Appendix 3
(Document 3)

Training
Appendix 4
(Document 4)

Renewal Safeguarding of employment
Appendix 1: settlement
(Document 1)

Phased working
Appendix 4
(Documents 4 & 5)

Participatory pension
Appendix 6
(Document 8)

Employee performance contribution
Appendix 5
(Documents 6 & 7)

Document 1: Result of negotiations from 12 September 1995

Between the negotiating committees of
Volkswagen AG
and the
Hanover branch of the metalworkers' union, IG Metall,

in the sixth round of negotiations the following result was achieved:

1. Agreement concerning the safe guarding of locations of company operations and employment

1.1 Collective agreement of 15 December 1993

The collective agreement on the 28.8-hour week, amended to exclude dismissals for operational reasons from 1 January 1996, and to set 31 December 1997 as the earliest possible date for such layoffs, is to be re-implemented.

1.1.1 The arrangements agreed on with regard to the division of working time have been changed as follows:

– Principle

The start and finish of daily working time, including breaks, and the distribution of weekly working hours over individual weekdays – as a rule from Monday to Friday – shall be agreed with the works council. Weekly working time shall in principle be spread equally or unequally but regularly on a shift basis over 4 or 5 working days, as a rule between Monday and Friday.

– Unequal division

• Under the annual scheduling and working hours plan, regular working time in production departments or production-dependent departments can be divided into a maximum of 8 hours per day and a maximum of 10 hours over and above the regular weekly working time from Monday to Friday.

• This agreed working time may be varied with the agreement of the works council.

• Those employees affected must in principle be given 2 months' advance notice.

• When working time is being divided in accordance with Volkswagen's flexible working week the 28.8-hour week must be maintained over the calendar year.

• An individual working time account may be introduced by internal agreement in order to ensure that regular working hours are adhered to over the calendar year.

– The provisions in Section 2.3 of the collective agreement concerning working hours – Saturday working – will continue to apply.

– Under works regulations, the provisions concerning the Volkswagen Week can also be extended by agreement to cover departments not dependent on production.

1.1.2 Equalisation payment 3 is extended for the duration of the collective agreement.

1.1.3 The provisions concerning overtime have been redrafted.

– Overtime arises when the daily and weekly working hours laid down under the agreed definition of the working week are exceeded. Overtime will only be remunerated if it has been sanctioned by the superior responsible. Only full quarter-hours worked will be included in the calculations.

– Extra payment for overtime under the skeleton collective agreement will only apply to hours worked over and above 35 hours per week.

– In principle, overtime shall be compensated with paid leave of absence from work.

Personal circumstances and company requirements shall be taken into account when the dates for paid leave of absence are agreed.

– Paid leave of absence for overtime may also be used as part of a phased transition to early retirement (progressive retirement programme).

– Paid leave of absence for overtime is paid at the salary/wage rate applicable at the time it is taken; further details (including shift allowances) are yet to be decided.

– If there is a compelling reason, employees are entitled to submit a written request for financial remuneration for accrued time credits.

Compelling reasons may arise

– where the employee leaves the company (e.g. due to dismissal, termination of contract, termination of employment with promise of reinstatement, etc.)

– in the event of foreseeable long-term suspension of employment (e.g. military/alternative social service, parental leave after the birth of a child, etc.)

– where the company is threatened with insolvency or is currently undergoing bankruptcy or composition proceedings.

A claim for entitlement arises in the above-mentioned cases at the time of termination or suspension of employment.

In the event of the employee's death his/her individual time credit is converted into a heritable financial entitlement.

The standard rate of pay at the time the entitlement came into effect is used to determine the entitlement.

– An individual credit account shall be established for the remuneration of overtime in the form of paid leave of absence from work.

The Volkswagen work credit is the instrument to be used for this purpose.

Arrangements will be set out in an internal agreement, which must contain the following as a minimum:

– The conditions, procedure and timing for determining the purpose of paid leave of absence for overtime.

– The procedure and period of notice for actually claiming paid leave of absence for overtime.

– The conditions and procedure for collective assessment of levels of claims for paid leave of absence for overtime.

– The conditions and procedure for providing financial remuneration for hours on employees' individual credit accounts where paid leave of absence for overtime cannot be granted for operational reasons.

– In exceptional and special cases, payment for overtime may be agreed with the works council. This applies to work in defined projects or in undeferrable cases (e.g. driving trials) and to work carried out by specialists. The parties to the agreement must be informed of such arrangements in order to prevent abuse.

1.1.4 In addition, the following clause is included in the agreement:

Where actual working hours in a plant (i.e. the total of regular working hours plus paid overtime) exceed an average of 35 hours per week per employee over the year, the company declares its willingness to examine the extent to which additional personnel can be recruited on fixed-term contracts.

The actual number of hours worked is assessed at half-yearly intervals.

The result of the assessment is agreed with the works council.

1.2 Collective agreements of 24 May 1994

1.2.1 The collective agreement on the model for "Phased Integration of Apprentices into Full Employment after Training" is being revised and will also be re-implemented with effect from 1 January 1996.

The following new clause concerning the integration of apprentices after training is included which, for the period of application, will complement Section 14.11 of the skeleton agreement:

"In principle, apprentices will be integrated into full-time employment once they have successfully completed their final examinations. In individual cases, different arrangements may be made on submission of a compelling reason and subject to the agreement of the works council."

1.2.2 The collective agreement based on the work-free block time model is being revised without any material changes being undertaken, and will be re-implemented with effect from 1 January 1996.

1.3 Progressive retirement programme

A provision will come into effect from 1 January 1996 setting up a progressive retirement programme to allow for a phased transition to retirement (part-time working prior to retirement). By way of compensation, a subsidy will be paid in accordance with the acceptability curve during the 3 part-time phases involved. Details will be regulated in an internal agreement.

1.4 Supplementary provision

The provision in Section 7 of the collective agreement on working hours – release from employment with a promise of reinstatement – is altered by means of a note in the minutes. Termination of employment with a promise of reinstatement can now occur even if none of the reasons laid down in the collective agreement apply.

The note in the minutes becomes effective on 1 January 1996.

2. Provisions concerning working hours

2.1 Flexible working hours

New provisions on flexible working hours come into force on 1 January 1996.

As in the past, the flexible working hours provision applies to the so-called "normal shift" and involves more flexible time arrangements without a formal time-keeping system.

On the basis of a 4-day week, the minimum working hours shall be 4 hours per day and the maximum 9.5 hours per day.

Further details concerning the starting and finishing times of the working day (within a maximum time frame of 13 hours), core working hours and a time credit programme (including arrangements for taking off time credited) are to be laid down in an internal agreement.

2.2 Performance contribution of indirect sector

From 1 January 1996 a requirement of 1.2 hours per week is agreed for the indirect sector (hourly-based pay/salary) as a contribution towards safeguarding employment. Further details shall be agreed between the parties to the collective agreement.

3. Principles of remuneration

New provisions concerning "hourly-based remuneration" and "performance-related remuneration" will be introduced with effect from 1 January 1996.

In performance-related pay, a work quota and/or regular manning level is agreed between the company and the works council on the basis of planning or reference data.

In the case of hourly-based remuneration, performance and performance targets are agreed between superiors and subordinates.

The complaints procedure for company, works council and employees applies to both principles of remuneration.

The version of the agreement which comes into effect on 1 January 1996 on principles of remuneration contains an appendix.

4. Common collective remuneration agreement

4.1 As a further step towards a common collective remuneration agreement, the following is agreed:

– The previous monthly wages/salaries scale is to be consolidated into a standard pay scale,

– "L-grades" are to be used for white-collar staff; all white-collar staff earning an performance bonus are to be regraded to the L-grade, and where the total of the efficiency bonus and individual bonus exceed the L-level, they will receive this sum as an individual bonus. This bonus will be adjusted accordingly for future pay increases and taken into account in collective provisions concerning payment. The collective agreement concerning performance appraisal and evaluation will not apply.

– In future, the L-grades are to be filled by experienced staff after a maximum time of 2 years grading in the basic salary group.

4.2 In addition, a committee with an equal number of employees' and employers' representatives will be charged with the task of formulating the new pay system.

5. Participatory pension plan

With effect from 1 January 1996 the capital formation contributions paid by the employer, which were previously earmarked for the types of investment permitted under the 5th law on capital formation, will be used as an additional (participatory) pension.

Transitional arrangements shall be made in hardship cases.

6. Amendments to the skeleton agreement

6.1 Section 3.2 of the skeleton agreement is revised as follows:

"3.2 Payment of supplement

3.2.1 For the duration of short time working the employees affected will receive a supplement to their short time pay.

The basis on which the supplement is calculated is the difference between, on the one hand, the net monthly wage reduced due to lack of work – based on the level of remuneration used for calculating the short time wage – plus the short time benefit and, on the other hand, the sum resulting from application of the percentage of the net monthly wage for full-time employment listed in 3.2.2 – based on the level of remuneration used for calculating the short time pay.

3.2.2 The net monthly wage used for calculating the supplement payable in addition to short time pay is shown below

Remuneration level	Salary group	% of Net monthly pay
A	5	95
B/C		90
D/E	6	87
F		85
G	7	85
H		85
I	8	84
K/L		84
M	9	83
N		83
	10	82
	11	82
	12	81
	13	80"

6.2 The following amendments to Section 4 of the skeleton agreement have been agreed:

6.2.1 The following text is added to Section 4.1.1:

"a 30% supplement for overtime (from Monday to Friday) will only be paid where the overtime exceeds one quarter of an hour".

6.2.2 The following text is added to Section 4.1.4:
"for Saturday working; 30%
for Saturday working
as part of a shift pattern 50%
and for Sunday working"

6.2.3 Section 4.4 is deleted without replacement.

7. Monthly wages/salaries increase

7.1 Monthly wages and salaries, individual monthly bonuses and equalisation payments will be increased by 4% with effect from 1 January 1996.

7.2 The same applies to the monthly wages, individual monthly bonuses and equalisation payments for monthly-paid employees who are on call and for members of the plant security staff and plant fire brigade.

7.3 Instead of a percentage increase, each employee will receive a lump sum of DM 200 gross for each month for the period August to December 1995, which will be paid in two instalments of DM 500 with his/her pay in September and October 1995 subject to the following conditions:

7.3.1 Employees will receive the full lump sum if they are in full-time employment from August to December 1995 and are fully entitled to a monthly wage or salary, continued payment for regular employment, holiday pay or remuneration for short time work.

7.3.2 Part-time employees will receive the lump sum in accordance with their regular weekly working hours as agreed in their individual contract of employment as a proportion of the regular 28.8-hour working week as laid down in the collective agreement. Payment of the lump sum will also be made in two equal instalments with their pay in September and October.

7.3.3 Where part-time and full-time employees are not fully entitled to payment of wages and salaries, continued payment for regular employment, holiday pay or remuneration for short time work for the months of August to December 1995, the lump sum will be reduced pro-rata.

7.4 In addition, the one-off payment specified in Section 3.2.4, § 2 of the collective agreement of 15 December 1993 is increased by DM 836 to a total of DM 1,600.

Part-time employees will receive the increase in the same proportion as their working hours laid down in their individual contracts of employment relate to the regular 28.8-hour working week as stipulated in the collective agreement.

7.5 Wages and salaries can be cancelled at one months' notice with effect from 31 July 1997.

7.6 Christmas bonuses as specified in Section 10.1 of the skeleton agreement amount to DM 2,000 in Group C in 1995 and 1996. The sums due to the other groups will be adjusted accordingly.

8. Provisions for apprentices

8.1 From 1 January 1996, payments to apprentices will be increased by 4% in the 2nd, 3rd and 4th years of training.

8.2 In addition, the lump sum specified in Section 3.2.4, § 5, of the collective agreement of 15 December 1993 is increased by DM 237 to a total of DM 455.

8.3 The collective agreement concerning the payment of apprenticesship allowances can be cancelled at one months' notice with effect from 31 July 1997.

9. Payments under other headings

The amounts payable under other remuneration arrangements specified in Section 3.2.6 of the collective agreement of 15 December 1993 will be increased by 4% with effect from 1 January 1996.

10. Implementation of the results of the negotiations

The parties to the collective agreement will agree without delay on the new texts of the collective agreements arising from the result of these negotiations.

11. Collective agreements on safeguarding employment

The parties to the collective agreement agree that in the case of termination, where there is failure to agree on any subsequent provisions, the normal provisions of the collective agreements (i.e. recuperation periods, 35-hour week including remuneration provisions and Section 4.1 of the collective agreement on the safeguarding of employment) will come in to force in their then valid form.

12. Stipulation prohibiting company penalties after strikes

The parties shall agree on a stipulation prohibiting company penalties after strikes.

13. Period for response

This agreement will become effective provided that it has been accepted by the negotiating parties by 4 pm on 28 September 1995.

Failure to respond implies approval.

Hanover, 12 September 1995

Appendix

For the negotiation committee of

Volkswagen AG

Hanover branch of the metalworkers' union, IG Metall

Note: for reasons of overall coherence, the appendix to the result of the negotiations is printed in Appendix 5, Document 7.

Appendix 2

The "Agreement concerning the safeguarding of locations of company operations and employment, of 28 September 1995" represents the renewal of the Volkswagen Model (4-day week) which was agreed in December 1993. The core elements of the agreement include: the safeguarding of employment through the exclusion of dismissal for operational reasons, the basic continuation of the 28.8-hour week and an irregular distribution of working hours (the Volkswagen Week).

Document 2: Agreement concerning the safeguarding of locations of company operations and employment, of 28 September 1995 including a note in the minutes on Section 7 of the agreement.

**Volkswagen AG
and
the Hanover branch of the
metalworkers' union, IG Metall**

have entered into the following agreement concerning safeguarding locations of company operations and employment

Preamble

The signatories to the collective agreement are agreed that the far-reaching economic and structural problems and processes of change occurring in society as a whole call for a new approach from both labour and management in order to solve these problems and safeguard employment.

Volkswagen and IG Metall are jointly pursuing the goal of safeguarding employment in the company's domestic plants and ensuring the competitiveness of Volkswagen AG. They are therefore continuing the system to safeguard employment in the form detailed below.

The parties agree that the arrangements should also apply to employees who do not fall within the scope of collective agreements. Volkswagen will take suitable measures to ensure that this happens.

§ 1 Scope

This agreement applies

1.1 geographically:
to all Volkswagen AG plants

1.2 individually:
to all plant employees who are members of the metalworkers' union IG Metall, with the exception of

– work-placement students/pupils
– students on vacation jobs
– graduate trainees

– students on internships/industrial placements

and

– employees on special contracts outside the scope of the skeleton collective agreement and the wage agreement, i.e. non-tariff employees.

§ 2 Working time

2.1 Working hours

2.1.1 Regular working hours are 28.8 hours per week as an annual average.

2.1.2 Under the collective agreement covering monthly wage-earners with a standby element and the collective agreement covering members of the plant security staff and plant fire brigade, the hours are as follows

– Monthly wage-earners on call
  * Nos. 1 and 2
    152 hours per month
  * Nos. 10 and 11
    148.8 hours per month

– Plant security staff
  * Continuous shift work
    133.86 hours per month
  * Alternating shift work
    143.46 or 134.85 hours per month

– Plant fire brigade
  * Continuous shift work
    207.2 hours per month

2.1.3 Under Section 14.7, § 1 of the skeleton agreement dated 21 November 1991 in the version of 26 July 1994, training time amounts to 35 hours per week.

2.2 Distribution of working hours

2.2.1 Principle

The start and finish of daily working time, including breaks, and the distribution of weekly working hours over individual weekdays – as a rule from Monday to Friday – shall be agreed with the Works Council. The weekly working time of 28.8 hours can in principle be spread on a shift basis over 4 or 5 working days, as a rule between Monday and Friday.

2.2.2 Unequal division
The Volkswagen Week

2.2.2.1 Under the annual scheduling and working hours plan, regular working time in production departments or production-dependent departments can be distributed on the basis of a maximum of 8 hours per day and a maximum of 10 hours over and above the regular weekly working time of 28.8 hours from Monday to Friday.

2.2.2.2 The agreed distribution of working time according to 2.2.2.1 may be varied with the agreement of the works council.

Those employees affected must in principle be given 2 months' advance notice.

2.2.2.3 When working time is distributed unevenly, the 28.8-hour week must be maintained over the calendar year.

2.2.2.4 An individual working time account may be introduced on the basis of a plant agreement in order to ensure that individuals work a 28.8-hour week over the calendar year as a whole.

2.2.2.5 Under internal plant regulations, the provisions under Sections 2.2.2.1 and 2.2.2.4 can also be extended by agreement to cover departments not dependent on production.

2.2.3 Three-shift working

Section 2.2.2 will apply, with the proviso that, as a rule, working time should not exceed 40 hours per week.

2.2.4 Saturday working

The provisions of Section 2.3 of the collective agreement on working time will continue to apply.

2.3 Holiday entitlement

2.3.1 In the case of a collective or individual 4-day week, entitlement to paid holiday, severe disablement leave and statutory study leave should be adjusted in such a way that it corresponds to the hours which would have been worked in the normal shift pattern on 5 working days per week.

2.3.2 Where working hours are distributed in accordance with Section 2.2.2, holiday entitlement as specified in Section 6.1.2.5 of the skeleton agreement will not be affected.

§ 3 Remuneration

3.1 Monthly wages/salaries

3.1.1 The wages and salaries to be paid include equalisation payments.

Equalisation payments and their amounts are calculated according to the relevant pay scales in collective pay agreements.

3.1.2 Equalisation payment 3 and equalisation payment 4 will be paid for the duration of the agreement.

3.1.3 Part-time employees and apprentices will receive equalisation payment 4.

3.1.4 Equalisation payments will be adjusted to take account of future collective agreement wage increases.

3.2 Remuneration arrangements

3.2.1 Basic hourly pay rates for hourly-based remuneration are calculated on the basis of standard remuneration rates and the 35-hour week.

3.2.2 For payment of length-of-service awards as specified in Section 10.3 of the skeleton agreement, calculation shall be on the basis of current wages or salary including the appropriate equalisation payments.

3.2.3 Monthly payments shall be made corresponding to the total annual bonus. The annual bonus as specified in Section 10.2 of the skeleton agreement will not apply for the duration of this agreement.

This also applies to apprentices and part-time employees.

3.2.4 Payment of the holiday bonus shall for the duration of this agreement and notwithstanding Sections 6.3.3 and 6.3.4 of the skeleton agreement, be as follows:

A portion of the holiday bonus is a component of equalisation payment 4 and is paid monthly. For the rest, employees whose contract of employment is not under notice of termination and is not suspended on 30 June of any year will receive a lump sum of DM 1,600 on 1 July of that year.

Disabled persons will also receive an additional lump sum of DM 676.

Part-time employees will receive a lump sum corresponding to their contractual working time.

The lump sum for apprentices is DM 455.

§ 4 Additional provisions

4.1 In order to safeguard employment it may be necessary for operational reasons to transfer employees temporarily or permanently. Each plant employee is obliged to accept any reasonable activity allocated to him/her. The parties to the agreement in the plant concerned will decide on the rules and procedures for assessing reasonableness. The main factors to be taken into account when assessing reasonableness are the suitability, training, previous job, earnings and place of residence of the employee concerned. Where differences of opinion arise with regard to the question of reasonableness, the committee responsible will take the necessary decision. If agreement cannot be reached, Section 18.2 of the skeleton agreement shall apply.

This procedure also applies where the employees concerned dispute the reasonableness of the job allocated.

Section 4.1 also applies where apprentices after training are taken into full employment in a different plant from the one in which they were trained.

4.2 Overtime

4.2.1 Overtime arises when the daily and weekly working hours laid down under the agreed definition of the working week are exceeded. Overtime will only be remunerated if it has been sanctioned by the superior responsible.

Only full quarter-hours worked will be included in calculations.

4.2.2 Extra payment for overtime under the skeleton collective agreement will only apply to hours worked over and above 35 hours per week.

4.2.3 In principle, overtime shall be compensated with paid leave of absence from work.

In principle, paid leave must be taken within 12 calendar months of the end of the month in which overtime was worked.

Paid leave may be taken at a later date if the employee and the employer agree on specific leave arrangements in accordance with Section 4.2.4.

Personal circumstances and company requirements shall be taken into account when the dates for paid leave of absence are agreed.

4.2.4 Paid leave for overtime may also be used as part of a longer break in employment or a phased transition to early retirement (progressive retirement programme).

4.2.5 Paid leave of absence for overtime is paid at the salary/wage rate applicable at the time it is taken.

4.2.6 If there is a compelling reason, employees are entitled to submit a written request for financial remuneration for accrued time credits.

Compelling reasons may arise

– where the employee leaves the company (i.e. due to dismissal, termination of contract, termination of employment with promise of reinstatement, etc.)

– in the event of foreseeable long-term suspension of employment (i.e. military/alternative social service, parental leave after the birth of a child, etc.)

– where the company is threatened with insolvency or is currently undergoing bankruptcy or composition proceedings.

A claim for entitlement arises in the above-mentioned cases at the time of termination or suspension of employment.

In the event of the employee's death his/her individual time credit is converted into a heritable financial entitlement.

The standard rate of pay at the time the entitlement comes into effect is used to determine the entitlement.

4.3 An individual credit account shall be established for the remuneration of overtime in the form of paid leave of absence from work.

The Volkswagen work credit is the instrument to be used for this purpose.

Arrangements will be set out in an internal plant agreement which must contain the following as a minimum:

4.3.1 The conditions, procedure and timing for determining the purpose of paid leave of absence for overtime.

4.3.2 The procedure and period of notice for actually claiming paid leave for overtime.

4.3.3 The conditions and procedure for collective assessment of claims for paid leave of absence for overtime.

4.3.4 The conditions and the procedure for providing financial remuneration for hours on employees' individual credit accounts where paid leave of absence for overtime cannot be granted for operational reasons.

4.4 In exceptional and special cases payment for overtime may be agreed with the works council (differentiates from section 4.2.3). This applies to work in defined projects or in undeferrable cases (i.e. driving trials) and to work carried out by specialists. The parties to the agreement must be informed of such arrangements in order to prevent abuse.

4.5 Where actual working hours in a plant (i.e. the total of regular working hours plus paid overtime), exceed an average of 35 hours per week per employee over the year, the company declares its willingness to examine the extent to which additional personnel can be recruited on fixed-term contracts.

The actual number of hours worked is assessed at half-yearly intervals.

The result of the assessment is agreed with the works council.

§ 5 Safeguarding employment

Dismissals for operational reasons are excluded for the duration of the agreement.

This does not apply to termination of employment for operational reasons in connection with socially acceptable measures (i.e. retirement provisions under a redundancy plan, other severance arrangements).

In particular cases, notices of dismissal resulting from a change in operational circumstances are permitted subject to the approval of the works council.

Volkswagen will agree on an appropriate statement for individuals who do not come within the scope of the collective agreements.

§ 6 Application of collective agreements

Unless otherwise specified in this agreement, the provisions of the other collective agreements continue to apply in their present wording.

§ 7 Duration of the agreement

7.1 The agreement shall come into force on 1 January 1996.

7.2 From 31 December 1997 it can be terminated at year end with 3 months' notice.

7.3 After such notice of termination has been given, the parties to the collective agreement undertake to commence negotiations in respect of a follow-up settlement without delay.

If the parties fail to agree, then the effects of this collective agreement will end 6 months from expiry of the agreement, but not before 30 June 1998.

In this case the normal provisions of the collective agreements (including Section 4.1 of this agreement) will apply in their then valid form.

7.4 As soon as this collective agreement comes into effect, the collective agreement of 15 December 1993 and the collective agreements of 24 May 1994 which supplemented it, including notes in minutes, are cancelled.

Wolfsburg, 28 September 1995

Volkswagen AG

Hanover branch of the metalworkers' union, IG Metall

Note in minutes on Section 7 of the collective agreement to safeguard locations of company operations and employment of 28 September 1995

The parties to the collective agreement agree that after notice has been served and in the event of failure to agree on a follow-up settlement the original collectively agreed arrangements (i.e. recuperation periods, 35-hour week including remuneration provisions) will come into effect in their then valid form; Section 4.1 of the aforementioned collective agreement will remain in force.

Wolfsburg, 28 September 1995

Volkswagen AG

Hanover branch of the metalworkers' union, IG Metall

The "Collective Agreement on Flexible Working Hours" includes an extension of the possible time frame which can be used by the workforce largely at their own discretion as part of the newly created working time autonomy (no more "clocking on").

Document 3: Collective agreement on flexible working hours of 28 September 1995.

Volkswagen AG and the Hanover branch of the metalworkers' union, IG Metall

have entered into the following **collective agreement on flexible working hours:**

Preamble:

The parties to the collective agreement agree that changes to the organisation of working hours are required, particularly in the indirect sector, in order to support joint efforts to bring about the necessary improvement in the company's competitiveness and safeguard employment.

In terms of the organisation of working hours this requires a flexible time frame to be co-ordinated between employees and their superiors, which can be filled by employees individually and at their own discretion, taking into account operational requirements and personal circumstances, in order to guarantee that tasks are carried out in such a way as to meet customer and deadline requirements.

§ 1 Scope

This agreement applies

1.1 geographically:
to all Volkswagen AG plants

1.2 individually:
to all plant employees who work the normal shift and are members of the metalworkers' union IG Metall, with the exception of

– apprentices
– work-placement students/pupils
– students on vacation jobs
– graduate trainees
– students on internships/industrial placements

and

– employees on special contracts outside the scope of the skeleton collective agreement and the wage agreement, i.e. non-tariff employees.

§ 2 Time frame

2.1 Flexi-time applies in the normal shift. Exceptions can be agreed by the works council for individual employees or groups of employees where this is required for operational reasons.

2.2 The standard working hours per working day amount to 7.5 hours for a 4-day week, taking into account the agreed weekly performance contribution of 1.2 hours.

2.3 Within the maximum 13-hour time frame to be laid down by internal plant agreement as specified in Section 3.1, each employee can decide when his/her own working hours start and finish in consultation with his/her superior and taking into account Section 2.4. This decision has to take account, not only of the employee's personal circumstances but more importantly also of the completion of the task in hand, the necessary co-operation with other organisational units and customer relations.

2.4 Minimum working hours are 4 hours per day and the maximum, is 9.5 hours (excluding breaks in each case).

2.5 Overtime is deemed to be any hours worked in excess of the standard working day as defined in Section 2.2 and which have been sanctioned by the superior.

2.6 Notwithstanding the basic principle to be laid down in accordance with Section 3.1, employees can arrange their days off from the 4-day week individually in consultation with their superiors.

Section 2.3, second sentence, applies accordingly.

In this case the number of days off which coincide with a statutory weekday public holiday (including 24 and 31 December) is determined by the company's basic guidelines.

2.7 The basis for calculating part-time pay is a standard working day of one quarter of the weekly working hours laid down in the collective agreement (7.2 hours).

2.8 Daily working hours will not be recorded by the company.

§ 3 Procedural provisions

3.1 Further details are to be governed by internal plant agreement; this applies particularly to

– the distribution of weekly working hours over the days of the week,

– specification of the time of the earliest possible start and the latest possible finish of the working day in accordance with Section 2.3,

– the duration and location of breaks as defined by the Law on Working Hours,

– the establishment of core working hours, where required,

– stipulations concerning the amount of time credits (redemption period: 12 months) and arrangements for their redemption,

– the form in which evidence of hours worked is to be submitted in accordance with Section 16, § 2 of the Law on Working Hours.

3.2 The works council is to agree on the establishment of working hours for the exceptions as specified in Section 2.1.

3.3 The works council may also agree to use different models for working hours for individual employees, groups of employees or organisational units, where this is required for operational reasons.

In this case, the standard working day should be adjusted accordingly, taking into account the agreed performance contribution of 1.2 hours per week.

3.4 The exclusion of individual employees from these arrangements for abusing the system of flexi-time or breaking the rules is subject to the approval of the works council.

3.5 Unless otherwise specified in this collective agreement, the provisions of the other collective agreements will apply in their current wording.

§ 4 Duration of the agreement

This collective agreement comes into effect on 1 January 1996 and can be terminated by giving 3 months' notice, but not before 31 December 1997.

Wolfsburg, 28 September 1995

Volkswagen AG
Hanover branch of the metalworkers' union, IG Metall

Appendix 4

The "Phased Integration of Apprentices into Full Employment after Training" involves the gradual progress of apprentices after training towards full-time employment in a number of "part-time stages", which are usually completed after three-and-a-half years. By contrast, the "Progressive retirement programme" provides for a gradual transition to retirement in 3 part-time stages.

Document 4: Agreement on the "Phased Integration of Apprentices into Full Employment after Training" of 28 September 1995.

In order to supplement and define in greater detail the collective agreement to safeguard manufacturing locations and employment of 28 September 1995

**Volkswagen AG
and the
Hanover branch of the metalworkers' union, IG Metall**

have entered into the following agreement on the "Phased Integration of Apprentices into Full Employment after Training":

1. Integration into employment

1.1 In general, apprentices are taken into full-time employment once they have successfully completed their final examination. In individual cases where a compelling reason is provided, a different arrangement may be made, subject to the approval of the works council.

1.2 Apprentices who have completed their training are integrated into a full-time employment relationship by progressively increasing their part-time employment.

They are generally integrated into full-time employment in the following stages:

a) Part-time employment of 20 hours per week annual average, from the time of acceptance until the 24th calendar month after completion of training;

b) Part-time employment of 24 hours per week annual average from the 25th calendar month to the 42nd calendar month after completion of training;

c) Full-time employment from the 43rd calendar month after completion of training.

The decision on working hours should take into account operational requirements and be made in consultation with the works council .

1.3 Where it is agreed that more staff are required, the parties in the plant concerned may make arrangements which deviate from Section 1.2.

The possible employment of apprentices on a full-time basis in the plant where they were trained may be agreed by the parties in the plant concerned for a maximum period of one year.

2. Mobility

2.1 Where appropriate, Section 4.1 of the collective agreement to safeguard locations of company operations and employment of 28 September applies to the employment of apprentices after training in a different plant.

2.2 Any apprentice who, on completing training, accepts an offer of employment in a different plant should be integrated into full-time employment.

In this case, Section 1.2 does not apply to the employment relationship on a permanent basis.

3. Final provision

3.1 Section 14.11 of the skeleton collective agreement does not apply for the duration of this agreement.

3.2 This agreement comes into effect on 1 January 1996.

3.3 The notice of termination, the earliest possible date of termination and the consequences of termination will be governed by the collective agreement to safeguard locations of company operations and employment of 28 September 1995.

Wolfsburg, 28 September 1995

Volkswagen AG

Hanover branch of the metalworkers' union, IG Metall

Document 5: Agreement on the "Phased retirement programme" of 28 September 1995.

In order to supplement the collective agreement to safeguard locations of company operations and employment of 28 September 1995

Volkswagen AG and the Hanover branch of the metalworkers' union, IG Metall

have entered into the following agreement on the "Phased retirement programme":

1. A progressive transition to retirement (part-time working prior to retirement) has been agreed upon.

2. The progressive retirement programme is subject to the following conditions:

2.1 Working hours in the individual part-time stages are as follows:
   – on average 24 hours per week
   – on average 20 hours per week
   – on average 18 hours per week

2.2 The decision to permit an employee to join the phased retirement programme will be taken by the company in the light of operational requirements and the employee's personal circumstances in consultation with the works council.

   Employees do not have an individual right to join this programme.

2.3 In the course of the phased retirement programme employees receive a monthly payment in accordance with the arrangements for part-time working as well as a gross allowance.

   The basis on which the allowance is calculated is the difference between the gross monthly part-time payment and the gross amount resulting from the application of the percentage of the gross monthly pay for full-time employment as shown in the scale below.

Remuneration scale	Previous pay scale/wage group		% of Gross wage/salary
1	A	5	95
2	B/C	5 L	90
3	D/E	6	87
4	F	6 L	85
5	G	7	85
6	H	7 L	85
7	I	8	84
8	K/L	8 L	84
9	M	9	83
10	N	9 L	83
11		10	82
12		10 L	82
13		11	82
14		11 L	82
15		12	81
16		12 L	81
17		13	80
18		13 L	80

3. Further details (i.e. age limits, duration of part-time stages, etc.) shall be governed by internal plant agreement.

4. This agreement comes into effect on 1 January 1996.

   The notice of termination, the earliest possible date of termination and the consequences of termination will be governed by the collective agreement to safeguard locations of company operations and employment of 28 September 1995.

   Where the contractual basis of this agreement is altered by the amendment of statutory regulations, the parties to the collective agreement will amend the agreement accordingly.

   Wolfsburg, 28 September 1995

   Volkswagen AG

   Hanover branch of the metalworkers' union, IG Metall

Appendix 5

As a contribution by employees to the so-called "residual costs" incurred by Volkswagen AG as a result of the collective agreement of 1993 it has been agreed that in the indirect sector employees should provide a commitment to improve performance by 1.2 hours (agreement on 1.2 hour standard performance of 28 September 1995) and in the direct sector to reduce the previous paid five-minute recuperation periods to a maximum of two-and-a-half minutes per hour (agreement on principles of remuneration of 28 September 1995).

Document 6: Agreement on 1.2 hour standard performance of 28 September 1995.

Agreement

**between
Volkswagen AG
and the
Hanover branch of the
metalworkers' union, IG Metall**

supplementing the collective agreement to safeguard locations of company operations and employment of 28 September 1995 and the collective agreement on flexible working hours of 28 September 1995.

1. A 1.2-hour performance contribution per week per employee for the indirect sector has been agreed in order to safeguard employment.

2. The weekly performance contribution is transferred to individual working hours accounts as a negative balance.

The negative balance can be cleared by one of the following methods:

– by using flexi-time to achieve the performance and clear the balance

– by performance at a later date

– by using days off or completed overtime to clear the balance

The methods used to clear the balance shall be laid down in the working hours regulations to be agreed by the parties in the plant concerned.

The performance contribution is deemed to have been achieved on paid or unpaid days off.

3. If through no fault of the employee, the negative balance is not cleared within one calendar year it will lapse automatically.

4. This agreement comes into effect on 1 January 1996.

The notice of termination, the earliest possible date of termination and the consequences of termination will be governed by the collective agreement to safeguard locations of company operations and employment of 28 September 1995.

Wolfsburg, 28 September 1995

Volkswagen AG

Hanover branch of the metalworkers' union, IG Metall

Document 7: Agreement on the principles of remuneration (LORA)

The following **agreement on the principles of remuneration** has been concluded between

Volkswagen AG
and the
Hanover branch of the metalworkers' union, IG Metall

as a supplement to the collective agreement on the principles of remuneration (LORA) of 18 December 1984 in the context of further developing the organisation of labour and continuing the process of improvement to safeguard locations of company operations and employment:

1. Performance-related pay

1.1 For tasks for which performance data can be established and specified the work quota and/or the standard manning level shall be agreed between the company and the works council on the basis of planning or reference data.

1.2 The performance requirements must be reasonable in physical and social terms and easily understood.

1.3 The stipulations as stated in Section 1.1 will be checked in planning and production try-outs prior to full production.

1.4 Once full production is under way the objective must be achieved through a process of continuous improvement. Employees, superiors, the works council and technical support departments will work together to achieve this objective. Any resulting changes in the work quota and/or the standard manning level must be agreed upon between the company and the works council.

1.5 The plant management, the employees concerned and the works council have the right to object to the agreement on manning levels and performance requirements, providing reasons, if they consider it unreasonable; in this eventuality Section 10 (including Sections 3 and 5) of the collective agreement on the principles of remuneration will apply.

2. Personal and rest breaks

2.1 Personal and rest breaks will be taken into account when deciding on manning levels.

2.1.1 Times and activities which offer a change of workload and a degree of relief from activities involving a regular rhythm may be added to recuperation time.

2.1.2 Down-times (i.e. due to technical faults, material shortages, quality problems, maintenance work, etc.) will be added to recuperation time provided that they offer a degree of relief from work and last for a minimum of 5 minutes.

2.1.3 Details of Sections 2.1.1 and 2.1.2 shall be laid down by an internal plant agreement.

2.2 Allocation of breaks in the event of failure to agree

Where no agreement is reached in respect of 2.1, personal breaks will be allocated on the basis of 3 minutes per hour and paid rest breaks on the basis of 2.5 minutes per hour.

Where breaks of up to 5 minutes per hour are required, payment will be made for 2.5 minutes of breaks per hour.

3. Hourly pay

The remuneration principle of hourly pay will not apply. Instead, superiors and employees in the sectors concerned will agree on performance and performance objectives.

The company, the employees concerned and the works council have the right to object to the agreement on manning levels and performance requirements, providing reasons, if they consider it unreasonable; in this eventuality, Section 10 of the LORA collective agreement will apply accordingly. (The procedure for lodging objections is being amended accordingly.)

4. Application of the LORA collective agreement

The provisions of the collective agreement on the principles of remuneration will apply provided that they do not conflict with this agreement.

5. Duration of the agreement

This agreement comes into effect on 1 January 1996.

It can be terminated by giving 3 months' notice, but not before 31 December 1997.

Wolfsburg, 28 September 1995

Volkswagen AG

Hanover branch of the metalworkers' union, IG Metall

Appendix 6

With the agreement on an additional company participatory pension programme, Volkswagen AG is entering new territory in terms of pay policy. The key point of the agreement is the conversion of the capital formation contributions previously paid by the company into a company pension fund.

Document 8: Agreement on an additional company pension fund (participatory pension scheme) of 28 September 1995.

Agreement on the establishment of a fund to provide a company pension programme (participatory pension programme) between

**Volkswagen AG
and the
Hanover branch of the
metalworkers' union, IG Metall**

1. This agreement applies

1.1 geographically:
to all Volkswagen AG plants

1.2 individually:
to all plant employees who are members of the metalworkers' union, IG Metall, with the exception of

– students on placement
– graduate trainees
– students on internships/industrial placements

and

– employees on special contracts outside the scope of the skeleton collective agreement and the wage agreement, i.e. non-tariff employees

– employees who will have reached their 55th birthday by 31 December 1995

– employees whose employment is terminated in accordance with the provisions of the 1994 retirement regulations and the associated notes in minutes dated 24.11.94 and 23.02.95.

2. In addition to the payment of wages and salaries Volkswagen makes a national pension contribution of

– DM 52 for full-time employees,
– DM 26 for apprentices.

3. Part-time employees are entitled to a pro-rata pension contribution, which is calculated as the proportion which their contractual working hours represent of the standard working hours under the collective agreement.

4. The national pension contribution is paid for each calendar month for which the employee is entitled to at least two weeks' salary, wage, apprentice allowance or social security contributions.

Where partial calculations of the pension contribution become necessary, the relevant statutory and collective regulations will apply.

5. Entitlement to the pension contribution will commence after 6 months' continuous employment with Volkswagen AG on the first day of the 7th calendar month.

6. The pension contribution over a calendar year will be converted into pension entitlement, i.e. into so-called pension units of the company pension fund, in accordance with the age-related pension scale in Appendix 2 of the Volkswagen pension programme (basic company pension programme).

7. Where employment ends before a pension becomes payable, the entitlement remains, provided that the deferment rules as specified in Section 1, § 1 of the relevant law (BetrAVG) have been complied with, i.e. if the employee has reached his/her 35th birthday and

- the entitlement to the additional pension contribution dates back at least 10 years or

- employment with Volkswagen AG or a Group company has existed for at least 12 years and the first entitlement of the additional pension contribution took place at least 3 years previously.

In this case, the amount of deferred pension payable from the company pension fund is calculated on the basis of the pension entitlement accrued on the date of termination.

Where relationship ends before the aforementioned conditions have been satisfied, the total pension contribution accrued since the conclusion of the contract plus interest at the current base rate will be paid out.

8. The granting of pensions from the company pension fund is also governed by the provisions of the company benefit programme as amended by the plant agreement which comes into effect on 31 December 1995.

Where an employee dies before the 5-year waiting period expires, the accrued pension contributions are paid to those surviving dependants entitled to receive them under the Volkswagen benefit programme, plus interest at the current base rate.

9. The parties to the collective agreement reserve the right to grant a further pension.

Individual contributions by employees may be agreed upon at plant level.

10. This agreement comes into effect on 1 January 1996. It expires on 31 December 2000 and does not continue to apply subsequently. No notice of termination is required.

The entitlement which has accrued by 31 December 2000 will be retained until the pension becomes payable or the employee leaves the company.

The parties to the collective agreement undertake to commence negotiations on a follow-up arrangement in good time before the agreement expires.

If no agreement is reached, the pension contribution will be paid in the form of a capital formation contribution with effect from 1 January 2001, provided that the collective agreement on capital formation contributions in the metal and electrical engineering industry which is in force at the time is extended beyond 1999 or continues to apply subsequently.

Wolfsburg, 28 September 1995

Volkswagen AG

Hanover branch of the metalworkers' union, IG Metall

The "Agreement on Short Time Working" is a further development of the "block model" agreed in 1994 and its provisions include short time working in connection with training, taking into account the so-called "degressive curve for benefit payment".

Document 9: Agreement on short-time working of 28 September 1995.

**Volkswagen AG
and the
Hanover branch of the
metalworkers' union, IG Metall**

have entered into the following agreement which supplements the collective agreement to safeguard locations of company operations and employment of 28 September 1995:

Preamble:

The parties agree that in order to safeguard employment beyond the reduction in working hours agreed in 1993, further measures are required to stave off the redundancies which would otherwise be unavoidable under the terms of Section 17, § 1 of the Law on Protection against Dismissal.

The main means of achieving this objective is through the instrument of short time working.

The parties have therefore agreed to make extensive use of the instrument of short time working within the framework of statutory regulations.

1. Scope

This agreement applies to the implementation

– of short time working in accordance with statutory regulations, provided that the short time working is used for training purposes;

– of short time working in accordance with Section 63, § 4 of the Law on Promotion of Employment (AFG).

2. Short time working in conjunction with training

2.1 Duration

For individual employees the period of short time working must not exceed 3 calendar months per calendar year.

A longer period may be agreed, subject to the approval of the parties to the collective agreement.

2.2 Allowance

For the duration of short time working the employees affected will receive a gross allowance to supplement their short time pay.

The allowance is calculated on the basis of the difference between the short time wage and the sum resulting from calculating the percentage of the net monthly wage for full-time employment, (see appendix) – based on the wage used for calculating the short time pay.

2.3 Period of notice

The employees concerned must be given 4 weeks' notice of short time working.

3. Short time working in accordance with Section 63, § 4 of the AFG

The duration of short time working is governed by statutory regulations. For contribution and period of notice, points 2.2 and 2.3 apply.

4. Final provision

4.1 This agreement comes into effect on 1 January 1996.

4.2 The notice of termination, earliest possible date of termination and the consequences of termination shall be governed by the collective agreement to safeguard locations of company operations and employment of 28 September 1995.

Wolfsburg, 28 September 1995

Volkswagen AG

Hanover branch of the metalworkers' union, IG Metall

Appendix

Net monthly pay used as a basis for calculating the benefit which supplements the short time wage

Pay scale stufe	Previous pay scale/wage group		% of Gross wage/salary
1	A	5	95
2	B/C	5 L	90
3	D/E	6	87
4	F	6 L	85
5	G	7	85
6	H	7 L	85
7	I	8	84
8	K/L	8 L	84
9	M	9	83
10	N	9 L	83
11		10	82
12		10 L	82
13		11	82
14		11 L	82
15		12	81
16		12 L	81
17		13	80
18		13 L	80

Springer-Verlag
and the Environment

We at Springer-Verlag firmly believe that an international science publisher has a special obligation to the environment, and our corporate policies consistently reflect this conviction.

We also expect our business partners – paper mills, printers, packaging manufacturers, etc. – to commit themselves to using environmentally friendly materials and production processes.

The paper in this book is made from low- or no-chlorine pulp and is acid free, in conformance with international standards for paper permanency.

Printing: Saladruck, Berlin
Binding: Buchbinderei Lüderitz & Bauer, Berlin